Alex Ja

Also by John Harding

FOOTBALL WIZARD: THE STORY OF BILLY MEREDITH

JACK KID BERG: THE WHITECHAPEL WINDMILL

FOR THE GOOD OF THE GAME: THE OFFICIAL HISTORY OF
THE PROFESSIONAL FOOTBALLERS' ASSOCIATION

Alex James

Life of a Football Legend

John Harding

 Robson Books

First published in Great Britain in 1988 by Robson Books Ltd,
Bolsover House, 5-6 Clipstone Street, London W1P 7EB
This Robson paperback edition first published 1992

British Library Cataloguing in Publication Data

A catalogue record for this title is available from the British
Library

ISBN 0 86051 492 7 (hbk)
ISBN 0 86051 838 8 (pbk)

Printed in Hungary

Contents

Foreword

I first met Alex when I joined Arsenal as a seventeen-year-old amateur in 1936 but I first saw him when I was ten. My father took me to Wembley to see the England *v* Scotland international of 1928 — the year of the famous Scots Wembley Wizards. The details are vague now but the impression James and those other brilliant Scottish forwards made on me remains to this day. It was an exhibition of football no one present could ever really forget.

Alex was certainly the greatest ball player I've ever seen yet what impressed me most was the apparent effortlessness and naturalness of his play. He once told me, 'I always knew whenever I'd played a bad game — in the dressing room afterwards I would be dripping with perspiration. If I played well, I would hardly break sweat.'

But Alex was more than just a great player; he was a kind, thoughtful man and a good friend. When I was on the verge of first-team football he told me, 'You're going to make it to the top — in football.' He knew little about my cricketing ability, you see. Golf was his only other sporting passion; indeed, he introduced me to the game and taught me the fundamentals at the South Herts Golf Club. All the subsequent years of pleasure I've had from golf I thus owe to him.

I managed to play alongside Alex on just two occasions during his last season at Arsenal in 1937. The first time I was at outside left, in the Bastin role with Alex inside. We played Charlton at the Valley in front of 77,000 people and in the dressing room beforehand I was very nervous and very respectful, addressing him as 'Mr' James. His advice to me was, 'You stay out on the wing, son, don't come inside and I'll look after you.' We beat Charlton 2-0 and I scored one of the goals. The old boy simply laid it on for me — it was so easy.

In later years he warned me about the perils of success. 'When you get to the top they are going to write all sorts of things about you, but never object. There will be indifferent comments and hurtful comments but you should take it all in your stride and always remember — if you weren't any good, they wouldn't be wasting their time on you.'

They never stopped writing about him, of course. He was a unique footballer and a wonderful man and I am proud to have been a close friend.

DENIS COMPTON

ACKNOWLEDGEMENTS

There are a number of people I must thank for invaluable assistance rendered over a number of years:

In Scotland: John Litster, who provided a wealth of documents and publications without which it would have been difficult to proceed, Alec Cowie whose reminiscences of James at Raith were also of enormous help as were those of Davie Collins of Ashfield, plus Mr Adamson, Kevin McCarra, Chris McCulloch, J. Soutter, Jack Finnigan and Motherwell District Library.

In Preston: Mr E. Griffiths at Deepdale, Mr William Knopp, Mr F. Hadley and Mr Harry Brownson.

In London: F. A. Spiller, Mr Peakall, Arthur Walden, Mr Iveson, Mr Stutchbury, Laurie Thurgood, Mr Case, Mr Hartley, the Rev. Charles Porter, John Burt, R. J. Browning, Simon Inglis, Phil Soar, Mrs Joy Stone and, in particular, Mr Bernard Chaplin.

In the North-East: Sid Woodhead, Fred Dodds and Hugh Gallacher.

In Derby: Anton Rippon and Andy Ward.

Many Arsenal players lent memories and photos: in particular I would like to thank Joe Mercer for his kindness and patience, also George Male and Jack Crayston, Tom Parker and Ted Drake, Jack Kelsey and George Swindon.

Fred Redding, Selfridges Curator, helped with fascinating research; Martin Watkins interviewed Peggy James in Australia; Steve Thomas talked of James the golfer.

Where Poland was concerned, Janusz Kukulski, sports writer, sent fascinating material and Mr Zbigniew Rzadkiewicz patiently translated it.

Charlie Chester, Alan Bartlett, G. H. Butler and Brigadier R. J. Lewendon helped with James's Army days.

Finally, I would like to thank the following members of the James family, in particular Joe Hill who has helped me for a number of years; Jim and Megan Murdoch, Audrey Muir, Mrs Peggy James, and last, but by no means least, Alex James's son and daughter – Alec and Patsy.

Alex James

Honours: League Championship medal 1930-31, 1932-33, 1933-34, 1934-35
FA Cup winners medal 1930, 1936

Club	Season	League		Int'nls	
		Mtchs	*Gls*	*Mtchs*	*Gls*
Raith Rovers	1922-23	25	5		
	1923-24	34	11		
	1924-25	37	11		
	1925-26	4			
Preston North End	1925-26	34	14	1	
	1926-27	39	11		
	1927-28	38	18	1	2
	1928-29	36	10	2	
Arsenal	1929-30	31	6	3	1
	1930-31	40	5		
	1931-32	32	2		
	1932-33	40	3	1	
	1933-34	22	3		
	1934-35	30	4		
	1935-36	17	2		
	1936-37	19	1		
Total		478	106	8	3

1

Old Mossend

In Scotland the iron-smelting furnaces that glowed orange and vermilion against the long and sombre Lowland winter nights, the coal-mines that ever further and more deeper burrowed beneath the Lowland surface and, above all, the great clanging shipyards of the Clyde, had been conceived and born by Scotland herself.
Moray McLaren, *The Scots*

My birthplace was Bellshill, an industrial township in Lanarkshire – not what you would call a health resort, but very dear to me.
Alex James in *Football and Sports Favourite*, 1929

THE ADDRESS AT which Alexander Wilson James was born on 14 September 1901 was Caledonian Buildings, Mossend. His father, Charles James, was yard-master at Mossend railway station and the family home – the end house in a single-storey 'but and ben' terrace – took its name from the railway company he worked for.

The Buildings were almost completely encircled by railway tracks, with branch lines and mineral lines snaking away to serve a score of ironworks and coal pits north and south of the main road from Edinburgh to Glasgow, along which the twin township of Bellshill and Mossend straggled.

In architectural terms, Bellshill was a typical Lanarkshire industrial community consisting of one straight street of solid, undecorative, mean buildings: a product of cold design rather than organic growth. No winding village streets here; no haphazard clutter of cottages clustered round a village church: Bellshill, in 1902, was the creation of severe, workful industrialism.

One of the principal architects of that industrialism – the revolution that had, in less than fifty years, completely transformed Lanarkshire in general and Bellshill in particular – was Colonel James Neilson. A year after Alex James's birth in the Buildings,

Neilson died at his palatial home of Orbiston House, no more than a mile away. His death came at the end of a period of almost unprecedented growth and expansion for Lanarkshire and Scotland, a growth in which the Neilson family had played a crucial role. But Colonel Neilson's death also marked the end of the 'romantic', individualist phase of industrial development when iron- and steel-masters – dedicated, ruthless, ingenious men – had become latter-day lairds, philanthropic feudal barons, dispensing to their millions of employees a rough mixture of education and charity, justice and back-breaking work. Their demise ushered in a faceless regime of ever-larger combines and conglomerates – English based – that eventually, when slump and depression arrived, were to remove what work remained from Scotland, and abandon its people to their fate amid a veritable wasteland.

No district in Scotland, possibly in Great Britain, suffered more than Bellshill from the economic slump that followed the First World War. It is customary to speak of the years that followed the financial crash of 1929 as the Depression, but in the industrial district of Bothwell that included Bellshill and Mossend, the term is applicable to the whole of the 1919-39 period. According to a social survey, almost 70 per cent of the male population of Bellshill was out of work in 1934.

So deeply has the Depression scarred the collective memory that it is sometimes difficult to believe that there was a time in the early years of the century when optimism about the future was the norm, when growth and expansion seemed as natural and inevitable as the Empire seemed invincible. In fact, the boy who would become famous as the footballer Alex James was born into a community that was experiencing a relatively prosperous time, when men were still arriving from near and far in search of work – if not in the ironworks, then in the coal pits or on the railways that served both.

The town that James grew up in was animated by an optimism that, though soured and severely tested by the harsh, primitive conditions in which men and women had to live and work, was never completely crushed. Their chaotic, dangerous existences, punctuated daily by sudden and terrible death at work (one of James's sisters was widowed by an industrial accident) or lingering, wasting disease at home, still possessed an energy that made life a thousand times preferable to the living plague of idleness that was to settle upon so many during the interwar years, when what had once been merely grim became squalid, what had once been austere became merely poor.

The slums where a kind of fierce if degraded life had once existed sank, after the First World War, into crapulous decay – a state the young James did not have to walk far from home to witness at first hand. Marion Street, the first turning off the main street leading from Caledonian Buildings into Bellshill proper, was once notorious for its Saturday-night brawls. Built to house steelworkers for the Mossend works in the days before the repeal of the Truck Acts, the tyranny of the Company store had merely been replaced by the trap of the ubiquitous public house.

Overcrowding and squalor at home drove men out into the numerous bars and drinking holes that were never very warm and welcoming institutions:

> bare, unfurnished as a station waiting-room, decorated only by the crudest advertisements for spirits and tobacco, they possessed all too often the air of furtiveness and unfriendliness imposed upon them by being the public places of sin in a small community . . .   Moray McLaren, *The Scots*

Yet even the pubs, as recalled by James many years later, reflected a kaleidoscopic, sometimes surreal world, a mixture of bizarre characters and unlikely tales, a hint of the many layers existing beneath Bellshill's forbidding surface:

> You see, Mossend Cross in the old days was better known as Sanny Miller's Corner. This was because Sanny owned the pub at the corner. Across on the other side, at the top of Calder Road, was a large vacant piece of ground – this was before the days of the Pavilion Theatre – vacant, that is, except for a two-storey building with outside stairways to the top flats. This Paddy's Castle and a tough joint it was, especially on a Saturday night when Sanny's pub closed at 10 p.m. Pub hours in those days were 8 a.m. to 10 p.m. every day except Sunday, and there was no closing for dinner or tea. The barman had to scratch a meal or two between pints. Pints in those day were 3d, half pints $1^1/2$d – and the popular schooner of beer $2^1/2$d. It was a common sight on Saturday nights to see and hear any number of the male inhabitants staggering down the village main street singing at the top

of their voices, quite often getting run in by the 'polis'.

Now, down the road from Mossend Cross on the opposite side of the road, just before I was born, was a drinking shop occupied by Dan Doyle. At the same time, Dan owned a second pub in the then Drill Hall building. Dan's name is known to few nowadays but back then he was very much 'to the fore', as they say. He was a famous full back for Glasgow Celtic and Scotland – one of hundreds of local men who were celebrities because of football. Sad to relate, Dan didn't keep his pubs many years. He started on the bottle himself and the inevitable end came.

There's a story told of Dan that, some years later, after his collapse, he was wandering about the East End of Glasgow – down and out – picking up a drink here and there on the side. He was in a bar one day when the man who was standing the drinks dropped a coin from his change on to the floor among the sawdust and got down to scratch in the dust looking for it. Dan, noticing the searching said,

'Whit are ye looking' fur, Wullie?'

Said Wullie, 'I've lost a thrupenny amang the sawdust, Dan.'

Said Dan, 'A wadnee worry ower much aboot it, Wullie, a've lost twa pubs, sawdust an a', an' it's no botherin' me noo!'

But if Dan Doyle failed, others in the liquor trade prospered: George and Missy Bruce's Snug Bar, the Auld Drum, Craig's of the Inns, Swann Inn, Charlie Kilpatrick's Auld Burly, Strathallan Bar, 'Pie' Murray's – all now long gone, their gaudy, affectionate names obscuring a grim social problem.

Yet to dismiss Bellshill as a drink-sodden hell-hole would also be very wrong. Alex James's home village was dear to him because it was much more than that.

As Moray McLaren has put it in *The Scots*, 'It was always possible from the main street of a Lowland Scottish mining village to lift your eyes from the grey almost majestic grimness of the main street to the equally grey and undoubtedly majestic freedom of the surrounding Scottish countryside.'

The countryside, of course, had given Bellshill its first life, and agriculture, even in the early 1900s, still helped to shape that life and the lives of the people who lived there.

During James's childhood, the houses lining the grim main-street concealed another world, one of muddy lanes and smithies (smid-

dies), dairies and bakehouses, orchards and stables – and the sight
of cows being driven along the main street was still commonplace.
Though rows of tenement buildings were encroaching upon fields
in all directions, Bellshill still retained its country past; it was a place
with a history of its own that owed nothing to Colonel Neilson and
industry. The 'true' history of the village was in its people and its
still thriving traditions: traditions such as brass bands, and master
bakers for which Bellshill was renowned across Lanarkshire.

The village had at least four brass bands at the turn of the century and in 1902 and 1905 Bellshill Town Band won the annual
championships at Edinburgh, plus gold medal for solo horn. Its
bakers were no less celebrated: Wullie Batters won the Diamond
Jubilee Trophy in 1901 for baking the best bread in Scotland – a
trophy already won by two other local bakers. Smith's, Marshall's,
Batters', and Austin's all sold their bread throughout Lanarkshire
and even beyond. In pre-war days the bakeries, just like everything
else, were still run by the men who had founded them and who still
gave them their individual character. There was, James later
recalled, one Wullie Smith, a stout, carefree, happy specimen of
Scottish independence who still baked from the old liquid barm:

> and in his locked store, so my elder brother told me, he kept seven
> large vats which contained his secret brews which did more than
> make good bread. If you had a hangover on a Sunday morning
> and were well known to Wullie you could get a speedy cure from
> one of his vats, which contained enough potent alcoholic content
> to put all things right with your world – but you had to be a close
> friend . . .

But it was not just for bakers and brass bands that Bellshill was notable in those pre-war years. It had its share of scandals too, as James
recalled:

> And one in particular I remember from school-days! There once
> stood close by Bellshill Cross on the main street a green-painted
> wooden structure used by an Englishman called Harry Treece as
> a photographic studio. In those days Harry was the only photo-
> grapher in the village, and for a few years did good business and
> made many friends. He was a very presentable chap, by all-
> accounts, with good manners and likeable personality and

apparently his great charm extended particularly to the young ladies of the community. Anyway, there was great public amazement when it became known that Harry was using his premises for wild parties with a number of the most prominent young ladies in the locality, and the chief relaxation appeared to be photographing the young ladies in all manner of poses in the nude! In the storm that followed Harry disappeared – no one knew where – and most of the young ladies did the same until the dust subsided . . .

In front of the studio was a thick telegraph pole where every evening the customers from the neighbouring pubs could be seen arguing and trying to span it with their arms. Many a bet was won and lost there – what's called making your own entertainment!

And yet Bellshill was fortunate, being on the main Glasgow to Edinburgh road, for many of the travelling shows stopped there:

My brothers – even my mother and father – had clear memories of the weird and wonderful entertainment that passed through. Bellshill's old pleasure ground was known as Bryce's Green, and old folk could recall huge bonfires being lit to commemorate Queen Victoria's Jubilee, and local yeomanry tilting at heads on posts.

There was something called Clark's Ghosts Illusions that visited the Green, which opened with a maudlin-sounding piece called 'Little Jim, or The Collier's Dying Child'.

Wombwell's Menagerie would come through on its way to Glasgow – elephants in Bellshill! And there were other first-class shows like Stevenson's Hairy Dolls, and the Tattooed Lady, and the Armless Wonder who could do anything with its feet that ordinary folk could do with their hands.

By the time James was born, cinema had arrived but live performers were still the principal attractions. In September 1902 at the Drill Hall, Dr Ormonde, King Hypnotist of the World, assisted by 'the World Famous and inimitable Ormonde family, the Bell Sunflower Company and a host of American and Continental artistes', was busy with his Great Hypnotic Clairvoyant Rosicrucian Psychomancy; the Oberammagau Passion Play, which was said to have caused men and women to faint with emotion was billed as cinematic support to Dr Ormonde.

Yet the shows and the pictures were intermittent things, providing rich memories and material for children's bedtime stories; the real passion play of Bellshill took place, week in and week out, on the makeshift fields and wasteland, on the streets and public parks. As Matt Busby, who was born and brought up in a collier's cottage at Orbiston, no more than a mile from Mossend, put it: 'The inhabitants were interested in having babies and looking after their menfolk if they were females; coal-mining and football if they were male.'

2

Carrying the Hamper

FOOTBALL FOR THE CHILDREN

Sir, The game has been and is being carried on very enthusiastically in our midst. At almost every corner you turn, boys are running up against you kicking at stones, tins, or anything else they can shift. In addition to this, most of them have learned to use very unbecoming language . . . It is an easy step from football to swearing and from swearing to the public house.

Letter to the *Bellshill Speaker*, September 1903

THE STRUGGLE AGAINST drink was waged in fierce terms from the late 1890s until the First World War, and with good reason. The consequences of excessive alcohol consumption were visible for all to see in the streets and alleys of any industrial town in Great Britain.

That football should have been implicated in the spread of drink is not surprising. Apart from the direct involvement of brewers as directors or financiers of many of the newly burgeoning professional clubs, the whole social phenomenon of crowds of working men caught up in enthusiastic rivalry, betting, celebrations, conflict and spirited argument was suspect to those desirous of social reform, of leading working people into more sober and creative – even religious – habits. Despite the fact that the game had, by the early 1900s, established a firm grip on the imagination of working men, it was still regarded with suspicion by those born half a century earlier.

For a parent such as Charles James, born in 1860, a church-going, abstemious man, it was barely understood as a possible source of recreation, let alone enjoyment. In an article published in *Topical Times* of May 1929, Alex James explained:

'My father was emphatically not a football enthusiast – if I had as many caps as I'd had lickings for playing football, I'd retire tomorrow. But I had all the moral support I could possibly desire from elder brother Charlie. It was to his sympathy and help that I turned in times of stress and doubt which followed the aforementioned lickings.

Charles James was 43 years old when Alex was born; a man of strict principles and habits, with a responsible position on the railway, and five children already past school age, he was not going to find another young son that much of a novelty in his life. Alex, however, with two older sisters, and three brothers, one of whom doted on him, never felt deprived of love or affection – quite the opposite. The strictness of his father was more than compensated for by the spoiling he received from the rest of the family.

Charles James was no tyrant, however. The family of which he was the head was, by all accounts, an extremely close-knit and happy one, loyal, with high standards in terms of both dress and behaviour. The Jameses had, it was said, a definite style about them, a respectability, and with always more than just one wage-earner in the family they were able to sustain a reasonable standard of living through slump and prosperity.

The family home in Caledonian Buildings was the single-storey 'but and ben' structure unique to Scotland. A corridor ran from front door to back, and off it were two rooms: kitchen/living-room and bedroom. Set into the walls of the living-room were extra beds, brought into use at night, covered by a curtain by day. Toilets were outside in the backyard, which also contained a shed for coal, bicycles and pets. An alleyway separated each house from the next, but the front doors were always open and families mingled freely. The houses were built for railway workers and as long as the wage-earner was alive, the family could remain.

Alex James was born and brought up in the Buildings: his father was eventually to die there. The eldest son, also Charles, followed his father on to the railway: they were a 'railway family' with an uncle an official in Holytown, just along the line from Mossend.

Mr James claimed that his people had, many years before, originated from North Wales and had gradually worked their way up to Scotland. If the story is accurate, any trace of Welsh culture had long since disappeared. His wife, born Jane Barrie Wilson hailed from Dundee, and Charles himself was a member of a local workingmen's Burns Club; a devotee of Burns, he was able to quote the bard at length – which he was wont to do at Hogmanay.

Alex's other brothers, Wilson and William, were both resourceful individuals. Wilson, said to be something of a rogue who enjoyed a good time, had a series of jobs; he was a butcher, then a grocer, and finally ended up running his own coal-merchant's business in Edinburgh. William, closest in age to Alex, after a spell in the Army during the First World War, was by turns a railway worker, a steelworker and then, after a brief period out of work, a breadroundsman for the famous Austin's bakery, a job he held until his retirement.

Only the two daughters, Mary and Christina, could be said to have struggled in life: both married steelworkers and both were widowed early. Mary lost her husband in an industrial accident soon after their children had been born, and Christina lost hers to illness before he was 40. Mary took her children back to Caledonian Buildings and there she looked after her ageing parents until they died: mother Jane in 1924, father Charles in 1928.

Charlie was probably the most successful of their sons in terms of employment. A clever child who won prizes at school, he was prevented from moving to the Upper School by the family's pressing need for an extra wage. He joined the railway, eventually reaching executive level. He was said to be a keen footballer as a young man and a good one, too, but there could be no question of his pursuing the game except as an occasional recreation. Hence, no doubt, his encouragement of, and enthusiasm for, Alex's sporting ambitions:

> If it had not been for him, I doubt if I should ever have been a footballer at all. Whenever I went home with my boot toes kicked out in those grand days as a kid it was Charlie who tried to soothe Dad down . . . he has often told me that he knew I was going to become a footballer.

Charlie's influence on Alex's career went further than simply acting as a buffer between the young boy and his sometimes exasperated middle-aged father. Charlie's belief, a mixture of wish-fulfilment and sublimated personal ambition, sustained Alex through a period when it seemed he might fail in his dream of breaking into the big time.

Alex had, very early on, more or less abandoned his school studies and was regularly in trouble with the school inspectors. But beneath the cocky bravado was a young man who could be easily hurt and discouraged, rather more easily than subsequent events in his life might suggest. As a football partwork published 20 years after his death put it, 'He was a natural showman who loved to entertain. Perhaps that explains the two versions of his abbreviated Christian name, always the affectionate Alec at Preston, Alex during his later years of glory and triumph. He was proud enough of Alexander "as long as ye shorten it to Alec, which is ma fancy, or Alex".'

There seemed at one time to be, despite his father's strictures and tannings, a definite danger that Alex might have gone 'off the rails' had Charlie not been around to counsel and to warn. All through his career, there would appear men who would sustain and encourage him, even protect him; he inspired a certain devotion. And no one was more devoted than brother Charlie. Good-natured, tolerant and generous with a great sense of fun, he became almost a second father to Alex in his schoolboy and teenage days.

When I got my first chance to play for my school, Bellshill Academy, as a youngster of 10 or 11 years old, Charlie was so bucked that he went out and bought me my first pair of football boots. What a thrill I got out of them! They cost Charlie four and elevenpence and I remember how I used to show them around to the other kids. They had what we call 'concrete toes' and those toes alone lifted me above the rest of the lads.

But Alex needed that extra peg. In a land of traditionally small men, Alex James was one of the smallest. Yet unlike many of his fellow countrymen he had no compensatory bulk; he was slightly built, as a glance at the family portrait will confirm.

My big trouble as a boy and even later in life was my lack of ounces and inches. Dad used to say, 'There's not enough fat on wee 'Eck to fry an egg.' He was right. However, I had ideas about that. I got to thinking this way. If I can work that ball well enough with my feet I shall be able to dodge whenever anyone tried to bump me – and I shall still have the ball! So I went out every day of my school-days with that idea. I was going to play real football until some team came along and said, 'This good wee 'un is better than most good big 'uns'.

It didn't work though, at least not for years after I'd left school.

The struggle to make the grade as a professional and the heartache it caused would be compounded by the ease with which another precocious young player, Hughie Gallacher, a close school friend, would find fame and football fortune almost instantly upon leaving school.

Hugh and I hit it off right from the start. We scrapped together and dogged together [played truant] and we romped the streets together . . . the two of us would do anything for a game. Many a time my dinner-hour at home consisted of a 'run around the table, a kick at the cat and out again' so that I could get away to play.

The snag was finding a ball. They were as scarce as gold to us. So we used to spend three ha'pence for a sheet of paper with verse printed on it and then go round from door to door trying to collect pennies.

I remember the sheet I had to take round had this verse:

'Please help our little football team
Although it's very small
Every penny you put in
Will help to buy a ball.'

I wonder if the boys up there are still trying to get pennies that way. I can sympathise with them if they are. I walked many a weary mile with that sheet of mine clutched in a dirty hand. Still, they were grand old days . . .

The subsequent football fame, not to say immortality, of both James and Gallacher led journalists to play up the 'school pals' connection until it took on an almost mythical quality, with endless invented anecdotes and incidents involving the two. There, no doubt, existed a bond between them as young boys based on a common love for and tremendous skill at the game, but psychologically the two were poles apart.

Gallacher was born in Bellshill on 2 February 1903, 18 months after James. He shared with James, as a Protestant, a particular 'attitude' towards Catholics, although in Gallacher's case, with parents from Ulster who were members of the local Orange Lodge (which led to controversies later on in his career as to whether he was of Irish nationality) the attitude was bound to be more intense.

Gallacher married, somewhat surprisingly, a Catholic girl from Bellshill, something which cannot have made his home circumstances particularly congenial. And the religious dimension certainly played a greater part in his life than it did in James's. When Gallacher visited friends in Belfast at the height of his career, someone actually took a pot-shot at him, the bullet hitting the wall just above his head. The death of his first child, from an early marriage which eventually foundered, cannot have helped his peace of mind but, then, as Hugh Taylor has said in his book, *Great Masters of Scottish Football*, 'His was an ill-starred life, alas'. Omens were always inauspicious: Gallacher wrote of his first breakthrough into the big-time, his signing for Airdrieonians:

> Imagine my surprise when the car drew up at an undertaker's office near Airdrie Cross. 'Queer place this,' I thought, 'to do football business' . . . and there in the vicinity of wreaths and other mournful paraphernalia, I signed the documents that really put my foot on the ladder of football fame.   17 May, 1931

Gallacher was an intense, moody man, always liable to blow his top on the field of play and often during the course of a game he would jeer, snarl and verbally insult opponents. He was certainly regularly and viciously fouled (as was Alex James: both men's legs were permanently scarred, and for much of the season bruised black and blue); yet perhaps the ferocity of the tackling on Gallacher was due to his taunting. In so many ways he was his own worst enemy yet, as Bob Crampsey has said in *The Scottish Footballer*, 'It's a curious quirk of the Scots character . . . that absolute idolatry has often been reserved for the troublesome players, and to these the nation opens its heart.' Gallacher's was certainly a troubled character, his brilliant career dogged by controversy and misfortune. To the outsider, at least, he would seem to have been more a natural product of the dour Lowland landscape than was his friend Alex James. This countryside, naturally sour and joyless, produces, according to Moray McLaren, 'men severe in aspect, restrained in manner . . .

with a celebrated laconic taciturn manner that can verge on down-right rudeness . . .'

In a series of memoirs in the 1930s, James commenced: 'Let's start by saying straight away that I have been the luckiest footballer in the world . . . Luck in this way: My whole career has been marked by the good fortune of having great friends to help me.' As a young boy, one of those friends was Gallacher and though their paths would soon diverge, they would remain good if distant friends, destined to share in much glory, if in little else.

And yet, in the beginning, it seemed that Gallacher led the charmed life where football was concerned.

3

A Cannibal Isle

I got a job at Beardmore's Mossend Steelworks at 6s 1^1/2d a week. It didn't last long.   Alex James in the *News of the World*, 1937

WHEN HIS SCHOOL-DAYS ended in 1916, Alex James had little interest in learning a trade, though no choice but to get a job. His principal aim in life was to become a player with Bellshill Athletic, the local Junior League team. Only in that way could he hope to progress upward to professional football. Bellshill Athletic was a particularly strong side with a proud history; in 1919 it would win the Lanarkshire Junior Cup, the 'Blue Riband' of Junior football in the area and the team would drive home in state in a suitably decorated motor-coach. Bellshill had produced scores of successful League players, many finding their way into English football – the ultimate dream.

For James, however, such ideas were a long way off. For now, fresh from school and with a World War raging, work was unavoidable: he joined the workforce of the Beardmore Steelworks, Neilson's old plant, which had been pressed into service during the war as a munitions factory, and was nicknamed 'The Projectile'. James, always the joker, found ways of making the time pass with a bang:

> Some of the lads at the steelworks had a bright little trick to pass the spare time. We would get an empty beer-bottle, put acid in it and then add some high explosive. There was just time to run, before the whole thing went up like a bomb with a colossal bang. We thought that great fun. One day the bottle didn't go off after we had dashed for cover so I went back, picked the thing up and gave it a shake. It went off all right, and I nearly went with it. The bottle exploded in my face; a chunk of glass covered with acid hit me in the cheek and stuck there. I yelled like mad and pulled

it out right away. A good job I did, too, for had I left it there the acid might have eaten half my face away in a few seconds.

James carried the scar on his right cheek for the rest of his life. More pressing, however, was the necessity to get another job. 'The Bomb-thrower', as he had been nicknamed, was given the sack. There followed a series of half-hearted attempts to hold down jobs – each of which ended, according to James, with his getting the sack.

Apart from football, I have never been able to keep a job. Dad was on the old Caledonian railway . . . and through his influence I was started there at 13s a week as a checker. I stayed a short time and then, for the good of the railway, was fired.

When he did earn money, he was less than conscientious in taking it home:

They paid us our wages in a tin containing a strip of paper show-ing in pencil the amount that we had earned. That was fine! We used to play cards on pay night and, if we lost, all that had to be done was to rub out the figures on the slip, write in another amount, much less, then take the paper home and tell my parents I hadn't earned so much that week.

Needless to say, he fooled no one, least of all his father. Unfortu-nately, his attempts to join a football club were equally unsuccess-ful.

All the time I was 'scroonging aroond' the local football club, Bellshill Athletic, trying to get a game. The players laughed at Hughie and me. 'You want to play for the "Hull?" You couple of shrimpies? Y're too wee!' they would say to us.
So we had to be content with pushing the club hamper of togs to and from the station for away matches. They paid us half a crown for that.

In fact, both James and Gallacher were managing to 'scroonge' games with the many more likely juvenile sides that flourished in and around Bellshill and Mossend. With so many coal-mines still in operation, there was a score or more of tiny communities within walking distance where a likely youngster could get a game – sometimes with expenses thrown in. Gallacher was soon picked for Tannochside Athletic, a village team a couple of miles to the west of Bellshill. Then Hattonrigg Thistle, a colliery side no more than a few hundred yards from where he lived, offered him a chance. James, however, had to be content with local park sides.

I was chosen for a Bellshill juvenile side, Brandon Amateurs, who used to play in a local tourney . . . I thought Bellshill Athletic were certain to take me out of Brandon and make me a real star, but they didn't. Nothing would convince them that I was big enough to play in their class of football.

Though Gallacher and James were of about equal height and weight, Gallacher had one crucial advantage over his school pal. Gallacher, from the very start of his footballing days, was a prolific goal-scorer. From his first games at school, goals had come in twos, threes – even sixes! Thus he was always going to catch the eye of even the least astute scout or talent-spotter.

Gallacher was also well suited to the rough and tumble of the forward line. Indeed, it is said that he originally intended to become a boxer and he was a close friend of two of the area's most illustrious boxing sons, Tommy Milligan and Johnny Brown. Gallacher might well have made a good little boxer; Bellshill produced them like it produced footballers. James, on the other hand, was less overtly aggressive and tended to play most of his football behind the forward line. He had been centre-half for his school team at a time when centre-half was the creative hub of the team, prompting attacks and linking forwards with defenders. It was an arduous role to have to perform in the hurly-burly of park football and it was not easy for a player, particularly one of small stature, to stand out. James's continued references to the scorn with which his attempts to gain selection were greeted is an indication that, though he was clearly naturally talented, few observers felt he could physically impose himself on the game as a centre-half. Convincing people was going to be a problem throughout his long career, whether it was at Raith Rovers, Preston North End or even Arsenal.

Gallacher found no such problems. Within a short time of signing on for Hattonrigg Thistle, Bellshill Athletic changed their mind and signed him up. He immediately started to score goals. It was a frustrating time for James:

> Hughie went on to get all the junior caps that first season. And I was still the hamper boy with no team at all. That was about the worst blow of all, to find my younger pal making progress when I was still idle. I've had one or two bad periods since turning professional . . . but I don't think I ever took them as I did that youthful experience.

Worse was to follow. Gallacher's Bellshill exploits had lifted him on to quite a different plane. League clubs were now regularly enquiring after him, Airdrie in particular. James was even present on the occasion when John Weir, a colliery contractor who was the financial power behind the Broomfield Park club, expressed an interest in talking terms with Gallacher.

However, it was a Western League club, Queen of the South, which had just turned professional, that came in first with an offer to Gallacher – of £5 a week! In 1920, that was a considerable sum of money.

Alex James had no such early cash bonanza, but his luck did eventually begin to change:

The supporters of the Cannibals, the junior team for which Alec James once played, did not like it when a famous talent-hunter came to watch Alec perform. So they set on the unfortunate "scout," as shown above!

Here you see wee Alec accosted by a complete stranger, and asked if he would like to join a REAL football club!

Things were at their worst for me when the secretary of a second-class juvenile outfit called Orbiston Celtic publicly said I might be worth a trial. That was enough for me. I didn't rest until I got it.

The captain of the Orbiston team took a liking to James: 'I must have done well, too, for after the game, Tommy Rogers, Orbiston's "tough guy", came to me and said, "You're going to play for us next season".' Orbiston was, in James's words,

> just a couple of rows of colliery houses and a football pitch. We used to strip in the communal wash-house. When we went down to the ground some distance away the place was never locked up. It wasn't necessary, for none of us had any money to leave in our pockets and our clothes would have elicited a sneer from any respectable rag and bone man.

Orbiston was a hard, uncompromising place. Matt Busby was just 10 years old when James came to play in his home village:

> In a village of 32 houses people can become clannish. That is why an outsider causing trouble to one household immediately invites retaliation from the 31 other families.
>   In local soccer circles Orbiston had quite a reputation. In fact, our village was popularly known as Cannibal Island, on account of the danger facing visiting teams there. Actually, the visitors were never in any danger . . . provided they lost. It is not a tall story when I say that a team which beat us on our own ground invariably had to run for dear life as soon as the referee blew his whistle at the end of 90 minutes. They might leave with two points but never with shoes and trousers.   *My Story*

Matt Busby was a miner's son, although by 1919 his father, along with all the other Busby menfolk, had died in France during the First World War. Left to bring up young Matt and his three sisters, his mother worked at the pit top and later at the steelworks in Mossend. Years later, when Busby was about to make his second-team debut against Preston North End, Alex James, then an established Preston star, visited him in his dressing-room to wish him luck. Busby had been hamper boy back in the days when James had first stepped out for Orbiston; indeed, James had been Busby's boyhood hero.

The music-hall style jokes about the Cannibal Island concealed a harsher reality. Busby's recollections of life in Orbiston are tinged with an understandable bitterness:

> Our house was no better and no worse than the others in the

village: two rooms were surely sufficient for a mother and father and four children. A bathroom was a luxury reserved for wealthy folk who, after all, could make themselves no cleaner in such surroundings than did the Busby family with a bucket of water on the stone kitchen floor. That bucket performed marathon service every evening when Dad arrived home clothed in colliery grime.

My Story

To talk of football might seem frivolous in the face of such hardship, when human beings had to live in damp, bug-infested hovels, when men had to walk home soaked to the skin and covered in grime because there was no pit-head bath and where families had to share a dry, midden privy in a communal backyard. But as Busby said, if you were a man, football was all there was to break the monotony; it is no wonder results were taken so seriously.

And it was into such an unprepossessing atmosphere that wee Alex James was pitched:

Yet it was at Orbiston – funny, tough, dirty little Orbiston – that something happened which set my feet on the ladder leading to every honour in the game.

The Orbiston crowd, tough though they undoubtedly were, took to me as if I were a ewe lamb. I was 19 years old when I started there, but I was still so small and frail that I looked perhaps a kid of 14 or so.

Tommy Rogers took me under his wing, and it was a case of heaven help any visiting player who did anything to me!

The result, according to James, was that he was able to play his own style of game without worrying too much about being physically roughed up.

My football developed and so did my skill . . . although away from home against some of the colliery teams was a different matter. I had to look slippy and those early games taught me the tricks I used to make the half-backs go the other way before I even touched the ball . . .

Just as important, he was seen by scouts and local managers and, as with Hughie Gallacher, the process, once begun, simply gathered pace. The first indication was the presence on the touchline of influential men in local football circles:

I was in the Orbiston team against Tannochside Athletic one terribly wet day. The ground was a sea of mud and it rained hard but I played well.

Lucky I did so, for 'Plummer' Laird, a famous figure in Lanarkshire and international football, and Johnny Bell, Portsmouth and Dundee star, were there that day.

Some weeks later, Laird was at another soccer match where he met Sammy Kyle, Secretary of Ashfield, an important Glasgow League side.

'There's a lad at Orbiston who might be useful to you', he told Sammy. 'He's only wee, but he has football in him.'

The first chance Sammy Kyle had, he came along to Orbiston to see me play. He must have been sorry that day even if he was glad afterwards.'

It was a Junior Cup tie against local colliery rivals, Hamilton Palace. The match ended in a free-for-all, spectators and players chasing one another across the pitch, but Kyle had seen enough of James to be interested.

A few days later I received a postcard asking if I would play in a match for Ashfield. Never so long as I live shall I forget the terrific kick that postcard gave me . . . I ran out of the house with it in my hand, I shouted to everybody I met in the streets. I raced up to the station to meet my brother Charlie coming home from work and I yelled at him, twenty yards before we met, 'I'm going to play for Ashfield!'

He was as delighted as I was. We hugged each other there in the street and half-danced our way home. Folks came out of their houses to look at us and laugh with us because by that time everybody knew about it.

'I knew you'd do it, 'Eck! I knew you'd do it!' Charlie kept repeating. It was a great day for him as well as for me.

A week later, Charlie escorted Alex to Glasgow and on to Saracen Park where Ashfield played.

4

Sojourn Among the Saracens

Sammy Kyle handed me an Ashfield jersey – miles too big for me . . .
Alex James in the *News of the World*, 1937

IN TERMS OF the friendly rivalry existing between James and his school pal Gallacher, the move to Ashfield had come at a most opportune time. Gallacher had just been persuaded to sign as a fully-fledged professional with First Division Airdrieonians – sealing his fate one rainy afternoon in an undertaker's office.

Ashfield, by contrast was only a Junior side on a par with Bellshill Athletic but it was a club with an awesome reputation – the aristocrat of the Junior game. And though it meant a 10-mile journey from Bellshill into Glasgow and then another trek out to the north of the city it was a tremendous fillip for James's self-confidence.

Davie Collins, the club factotum, 21 years old when James first arrived and still with the club some 66 years on, remembers the time as clearly as if it were yesterday:

I was a pattern-maker then in an engineering shop. The area around Ashfield was all foundries and my father was foreman in a factory, he was a boss . . . they called him 'the body-snatcher' in the old days, relating to his talent-spotting for Ashfield. There's a story about him and it goes, he was standing outside the Samaritan Hospital one Sunday morning and a fellow says, 'Hey Davie! What are you doing here?' And my father says: 'I'm waiting to sign on all the bairns born wi' a tossil!'

Alec got five bob a week to come and play here. Lucky! No bonuses. He would have to travel by tram-car to Uddingston, then get another tram-car into Glasgow. He hadn't tuppence. My mother would make scones and some of the players might come up to the house for a scone and a cup of tea – which Alec did. So Alec and I became close friends. 'Eck, we used to call him and I

The Cross, Mossend, at about the time of the birth of Alex James

The James family, around 1914. Back row; daughter Christina, sons Wilson and Bill, daughter Mary, Front row; Charles James senior, 'wee Alec', Mrs James, nee Jane Barrie Wilson, eldest son Charlie

The Board of Directors of Raith Rovers, 1923 – 24 – 25, Back row; J.H. Logan (Secretary and Manager), D. Hetherington, R.J. Morrison, J. Bogie; front row; A. Fraser, T. Smith, A.G. Adamson (President) G. Kilpatrick (Vice – President), Wm. C. Ritchie

August 1924; J.H. Logan, the manager is shown here with (back row) Miller*, Bell Raeburn* Mathieson, Hilley, Chester, McDougall, trainer Dave Willis and (front row) Jennings, James Cowie*. Barton, Morris, Moves, Ritchie, Turner, Slavin* (* part-time players)

was always 'Daik', after my father who used to go round the
dykes catching rabbits as a young man   the name was passed
on.
Alec was a confident fellow. Just the way he played on the park
you could see he was full of confidence. Just a typical wee
country fellow, hail-fellow-well-met! With his hair always parted
centre-shed, and big boots wi' metal tips, typical mining village
style.
But those feet were on the ground; he was always level-
headed. He and I got on. I gave him his boots for his first match
here and I said to myself, if he's as confident on the park as he is
in the dressing-room he'll need no telling. And he knew all the
answers. He was only with us for less than a season but you could
see, he stood out a mile from the moment he started. Great
thinker, a general: he'd lay back, dictate. He could look after
himself. I used to say, he's an old head on young shoulders. We've
had schoolmasters in our team and we've had miners – academi-
cally no comparison. But on the park the miners were the tea-
chers! Alec had a football brain. I'd say to him, 'Alec, you've all
your brains from your knees down! None in your heid!' I could
talk to him like that . . . but he had it all, even as a young man
and there's no accounting for that – it can't be taught!

Ashfield was just then on the crest of a wave. The previous season
it had won all three major Junior trophies: the League title, the
Maryhill Cup and the North-Eastern Cup. The *Glasgow Evening
Times* reported in January 1921 that 'matters are fairly booming at
Saracen Park these days!' With the money raised from large crowds
(regularly over seven thousand) Ashfield was able to build a new
stand – the first team in the Junior League to be able to afford one
of all-brick construction. But success brought with it inevitable
penalties.
    Until 1925, Senior Scottish League clubs could sign on Juniors
for no more than a nominal £5 or £10. Junior clubs might have nur-
tured, taught and invested time and attention on their players, but
the Seniors could take whomsoever they wanted.
    The result for Junior sides was a continual dislocation and dis-
ruption and, unfortunately for James, Ashfield was entering upon
just such a period. Having been spectacularly successful, they had
rapidly been stripped of their most valuable assets – players. The

club was now in the process of re-building and it would be another 16 years before the team would reach its present peak again.

I was with them the better part of the season and that was the only time in 18 years that they didn't collect one or other of the Scottish junior honours. And to be quite candid they were a poor lot that season. While I was with them, our chief occupation was getting knocked out of the various competitions.

Despite Ashfield's poor form (the team would finish close to the bottom of the Junior League) it was, from a footballing point of view, an exciting time to be in Glasgow even though on the periphery.

The two premier teams – Glasgow Rangers and Celtic – were struggling to achieve domination of the new soccer world emerging from the chaos of the War. If James had dreams of playing for either club he never revealed them. As a Protestant he would have suited Rangers, of course, but as a boy he had, along with Hughie Gallacher, been exposed to the influence of one of the great Celtic sides containing Charlie Shaw in goal, Joe Dodds and Alec McNair in defence with Jimmy McMenemy up front feeding the ball to the inimitable Patsy Gallacher.

Hughie Gallacher wrote many years later:

Guess where we went on Saturday afternoon? Glasgow Celtic. We kept our pennies for the match. Who did we watch? Why, Patsy Gallacher. We got many lessons from him. Alex used to watch his every movement. Those swerves, those eel-like runs, those rasping shots and that clever positional play. What lessons!

Patsy Gallacher was a perfect model for both young players, not least because of his size. The Mighty Atom, Peerless Patsy, who had replaced the legendary Jimmy Quinn, was never more than nine stone and stood just 5ft 6in. For small boys he was a figure of romance, gaining a place in the great Celtic side at the age of 17 and winning a Scottish Cup medal in his first season. It is interesting to hear what he considered to be one of the keys to his success:

It's all a matter of psychology. I always set out in the early stages to impress the opposition that I was the 'gaffer', that I played second fiddle to no man. Maybe in addition I had that extra sense

that enabled me to divine an opponent's thoughts, whether he
was in possession or coming to me in an effort to gain possession.

Anticipation, a sixth sense as to what might happen two, three
passes ahead, swiftness of execution: these can be watched but not
necessarily copied. But attitudes and a determination to succeed:
these qualities both young men imbibed from Patsy Gallacher.
James, in particular, was in need of such inner conviction:

> The members of the Ashfield committee were not unanimous
> about me. Some thought I hadn't height enough to carry me
> through successfully but, in the end, they came to the view that
> height is not everything . . . All this time I had a faithful friend
> in Sammy Kyle who never tired singing my praises.

Sammy Kyle had his reasons.
By January 1922, James had established himself in the side and
received occasional lines of praise from the *Glasgow Evening
Times:* 'From the centre-kick James had a brilliant run for the
visitors but shot over the bar' (7 January); 'James cleverly scored
for his team' (14 January); 'James was the outstanding forward for
Ashfield and all the danger was coming from the right wing' (4
March) – it was at inside right that he was playing for the Saracen
team. As he put it:
'I attracted attention on account of clever footwork. A good many
clubs were interested—' Indeed, in May it was rumoured that
interest had been shown as high up as Parkhead. Nothing as concrete as an offer emerged, however, until James received his first
representative cap: he was selected for the Glasgow Junior League
team in April to face Midlothian Juniors at Easter Road, the home
of Hibernian. As usual on such occasions, the scouts and managers
were out in force:

> 'Sailor' Hunter, Motherwell's manager, came to see me after the
> Edinburgh game. His proposal was perfectly straightforward. He
> would be ready to sign me on if I suited after the first trial,
> offering me good terms. For a time I would have to remain with
> Ashfield without pay, of course, but I knew I could rely on his
> word to sign me as soon as I was experienced enough.
> It suited me, but I didn't jump at it. I wanted to see if anybody

else was interested. 'I'm quite happy with Ashfield,' I told him. 'I'm not worried about moving.'

Accordingly I turned out for Motherwell reserves the next Saturday at Ayr. It was my baptism in Senior football. I'm not likely to forget it. Some of the players were niggling from the word go. It was no use trying to play football. Altogether it was the worst game I have ever played in.

The climax came when one of the players waited for his opponents to come out of the dressing room and 'sorted' them out one by one. An incident which cost him a £10 fine and kind of put me off Senior football . . .

Mr Hunter saw me afterwards and paid me a few compliments and suggested I ought to have another and fairer trial – next Saturday against the Albion Rovers Reserves. I was on, and when he further suggested I should drop in at the ground at night and put in a little training I was delighted.

On the Tuesday night, feeling rather bucked, I turned up at Fir Park. I walked in and found a few men knocking around. They gave me one look, saw a very small youth standing by the door and waited. I just didn't have the heart to say who I was and why I had come. At the end of half an hour, no one had said a word to me and I slipped away – and never returned.

An experience like that was tremendously disappointing and maybe I was oversensitive. If only I had dropped a line to Mr Hunter everything might have turned out differently. He never knew I had been at the ground.

Motherwell, of course, was the nearest First Division club to Bellshill – no further than a short tram-ride. 'Sailor' John Hunter was building a team that would, by the early Thirties, be considered one of the classic teams of Scottish football.

From 1927 until 1934 they would be in the top three of the Scottish First Division and would be runner-up four times. They would appear in two Scottish Cup Finals and in 1931/32 they would become Scottish champions, five points clear of Rangers and 18 clear of Celtic in third place!

That success was based principally upon a refusal to sell its best players to English clubs, a policy almost unique outside the Old Firm. Motherwell were able to make money attracting huge crowds wherever they went, thus making up for the fact that home gates, during a period of economic slump, rarely topped 10,000.

In addition to the policy of not selling was a determination to run the club along the most economical of lines. Not for it the financial wastage that characterised the activities of many of its country cousins. Motherwell players were paid no fancy under-the-counter bonuses and were content to play for weekly wages considerably lower than those received by men whom they regularly met and defeated week in week out. For it was their team spirit, fostered by such collective sacrifice, that was crucial to their outstanding success.

Motherwell, with its rigid set of principles where wages and transfers were concerned, would never, one suspects, have appealed to James.

But then, perhaps Motherwell would have been too close for comfort for a man who, all his life, demonstrated a desire for football adventure, even escapism. Bellshill was, in the early Twenties, rapidly becoming a town of industrial and social tragedy. The economic collapse had started and, in 1921, in response to the post-war decontrol of mines and the sudden rise in imported coal, coal-mine owners started moves to reduce wages by abolishing national agreements. A national strike was threatened, only to be called off on 'Black Friday', 15 April 1921. The miners, meanwhile, stayed out for some weeks longer.

In local coal-mining areas there was a great deal of violence; in Bellshill, Hamilton, Coatbridge and smaller villages ugly scenes occurred as flying pickets fought with police. Volunteer reservists were being marched into the collieries and in some districts there was even a curfew imposed by the police; anyone caught out after nine at night was liable to be severely beaten.

The following years saw strikes in the engineering industry, in ship-building and iron and steel, as unemployment soared. (In December 1920 the number of men out of work in Great Britain was recorded as 691,103. By March 1921 this had reached 1,355,000 and was over 2 million by June.)

The misery and gloom of the interwar years had started.

James, unlike his friend Hughie Gallacher – who was now trying hard to get into the Airdrienonian first team – had never been closely involved in local politics nor even economics, and escape must have seemed very attractive to him. So when Sammy Kyle offered him an opportunity, he was eager to take it.

5

A Coming Bobby Walker

The day I first met Mr R. J. Morrison, the Raith Rovers Director, was a lucky one for me. Frankly, I don't suppose I would be in the game today but for him. He helped me through my early troubles when I felt like packing up the game for good.   Alex James in *Thomson's Weekly News*, 1931

IN A SERIES entitled 'From Diamonds in the Rough – Famous Footballers and How They Were Discovered', published in the magazine *Topical Times* in 1929, Bob Morrison gives a brief insight into the motives of men besotted by football:

> I had been a great believer in the Bobby Walker style of play and I had been on the lookout for a fellow whose tactics were as near to those of the great Scottish international as I could get. It was by pure accident that my eyes lighted on the player of my dreams ... I saw visions of Bobby Walker in his play ...

Dreams, visions and the quest for a perfection glimpsed in youth and never forgotten – in Morrison's case that perfection had been Bobby Walker of turn-of-the-century Hearts of Midlothian, one of the players who joins men like Jimmy Quinn, Jimmy McMenemy, Bob McColl, Bobby Templeton to form the pantheon of early Scottish football greats, men whose faces once adorned the banners of 'brakes clubs', carried proudly aloft like pagan saints.

As early as the 1920s, such men were part of an Edwardian mythical land beyond the First World War, where stirring deeds were done and battles hard fought, cleanly won.

Set in the rather less than idealistic world of modern professional football, such dreams might seem more like delusions. Certainly

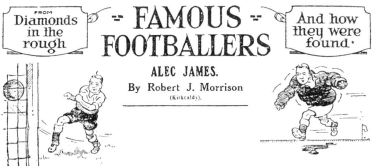

~ FAMOUS ~ FOOTBALLERS

ALEC JAMES.
By Robert J. Morrison
(Kirkcaldy).

the tangle of events that led Alex James to sign for Raith Rovers had one common thread: money. The love affair, in the beginning, was a one-sided one.

Morrison's initial sighting of James, however, had been pure chance: he, too, had been at the Glasgow v. Midlothian Junior League match:

> The fellow we were after was Johnny Borland, the outside right of the Glasgow Junior League eleven and Rutherglen Glencairn. I watched all the players closely but the fellow who always took my eye was the little inside right . . .

Afterwards, the Raith party discussed the various players on view, but there was some disagreement with Morrison's assessment of James. However, a week later, he established contact with James via 'a gentleman whose name I will not mention' (as Morrison coyly put it in 1929).

The 'gentleman' was Sammy Kyle and Morrison's reluctance to reveal his identity was due to the fact that Kyle, though secretary of Ashfield, was also acting as an unofficial scout for Raith Rovers – a breach of Junior League regulations. (After complaints from Motherwell a year later, Kyle would be banned from all Junior League activity.)

Kyle informed Morrison of Motherwell's interest in James and of the second trial match, and together they decided to intercept

James, summoning him by telegram to Glasgow to the Kenilworth Hotel. Out of the initial meeting came the offer of a trial for Raith Rovers reserves against Rangers reserves at the famous Ibrox ground.

> I can't remember much about that game except that there were a lot of sporting tussles with the Rangers left back. I know that crowd had a good laugh at me because the jersey was far too big and it made me look such a blooming kid!

James estimated that half a dozen other League clubs made enquiries about him following the trial. However, immediately upon Morrison's return from a close-season tour of Denmark, negotiations resumed in earnest at the Kenilworth Hotel. Morrison admitted, 'The little fellow knew what he wanted in the way of wages all right!' but, after several long sessions, a deal was agreed. 'We were agreeable to him staying in Glasgow but he decided to come and live in Kirkcaldy so all was well as far as I was concerned.' James too was pleased:

> Over and above wages I was to be on a bonus of £1 while I was in the first team – not that there seemed much chance of earning it for a good while. And a job was to be found for me in Kirkcaldy. I wanted something to fall back on if I should turn out to be a failure.

What was not revealed until many years later was that Morrison was to pay James a proportion of his wage out of his own pocket. Unconvinced as to his abilities or his physical strength, the rest of the Raith board would only agree to offering a basic wage. Thus, James was, in all respects, Morrison's 'baby'. Exactly what the 'job' referred to by James was to be, was never revealed; what is certain is that James never took up any other trade than football.

And, once signed, James quickly proved to be something of a 'prima donna': a mixture of arrogance, wounded pride and no little cheek. 'I was a cussed little fellow in those days', he later admitted, and he was sorely to try Morrison's reserves of patience.

The trouble began when he found himself unable to hold down a first-team place. When first signed on, he had not been promised that he would even play in the first team, but when injuries gave

A FOOTBALL FAVOURITE

James, Raith Rovers. One of the most diminutive inside-forwards in Scotland.

Few players are more dependent solely on skill, and still fewer can so completely overcome physical disadvantages.

A deceptive swerve, wonderful footcraft, and great power of ball control give James a most captivating style, and make him one of the strongest links in Raith's vanguard.

A youthful prodigy, who must have begun studying the game at the extremely early age of one, or thereabouts.

him his chance, he resented subsequently being removed from the limelight.

In the first four months of the 1922/23 season he was to play in just six first-team games. Doubts were expressed by the committee about his physique and, more seriously, about his attitude. His first-team debut could not have been more auspicious, however. On 9 September 1922, he was selected to play against Glasgow Celtic at Parkhead; the Celtic team included Charlie Shaw in goal, McStay and Hilley at full back and his boyhood hero, Patsy Gallacher, at inside left. Even the referee that day hailed from Bellshill.

The game was notable mainly for James's miss directly in front of goal. The *Kirkcaldy Times* reported: 'Had Shaw waited on the youngster shooting, the probability is that he would have been beaten. Showing fine judgement, Shaw ran out and James, in his haste to shoot, put the ball wildly over.'

Three more games followed, with indifferent results for Raith. Against Airdrie (and school pal Gallacher) the *Kirkcaldy Times* correspondent considered that:

> James was the outstanding man of the forward line and delighted the crowd with his clever centres. He showed a tendency, however, to hang on rather long on the ball and this made his play less profitable than it might have been.

After his next game, this against 'Sailor' Hunter's Motherwell, James was dropped. This should have been no catastrophe; only a year or so before he had been struggling in the mud at Orbiston's Cannibal Island. But he took the decision badly: 'I made no secret of the fact that I was feeling rotten about the whole business.'

Morrison attempted to rationalise and to argue: 'Alec had played seven games. This was far too much for a young lad of 17 or 18 years and so, as was natural, in the last game he came off the field very sore . . .'

James certainly lacked strength and stamina – indeed, the crowd at Kilmarnock had nicknamed him the 'wean'. Nevertheless, Morrison appeared to accept much of the blame for James's poor form and went so far as to pay him the £1 a week he would have been getting had he still been in the first team. James simply saw it as his rightful due: 'If I had done nothing to deserve being dropped from the first team, I wanted first-team wages, I said. I must have

cost Bob a lot of cash and more grey hairs while I was at Raith
Rovers!'

After almost six weeks in the 'A' team, he was brought back
against Third Lanark but, despite a spectacular goal, he once again
failed to impress the selection committee. He was dropped again.
In the reserves the following week he was considered to have played
badly and there was a move by some of the committee to terminate
his contract. Morrison persevered:

> He was only a boy and I had agreed to take a fatherly interest in
> him. I put in a plea for him to be persevered with and on the
> suggestion of our Chairman it was ultimately agreed that the
> manager give him a lecture and a few instructions on his play.

James later claimed that during the 'lecture' the hapless Raith manager, Jimmy Logan, had insisted that he alter his whole style of play,
that he 'run after the man in possession'. This, James claimed, had
never occurred to him before: 'I wanted to keep playing for Raith
but I didn't want to be bound by rules and regulations about what I
could or could not do on the field. What they wanted was
impossible.'

There followed a noisy row with Logan, after which James went
back to his digs and prepared to walk away from the game, there
and then.

But James had talked himself into a corner; in some ways, it had
been inevitable that something of the kind would happen ever since
he decided to make the 40-mile trip from the west to the east, from
Glasgow to Edinburgh and thence to Fife.

Indeed, travelling over the majestic Forth bridge with the spectacular but sobering city of Edinburgh behind him, he must have
felt at times that he was exchanging one entirely different world for
another. In those early days, he would feel much happier moving in
the opposite direction. With a sense of relief, he would leave behind
the steep and winding heights and hanging gardens of the New
Town. He would take the afternoon train from Edinburgh to
Glasgow to emerge from Central Station into the lamplit clamour
of Argyle Street, into the swarming Saturday-evening crowds
shouting, laughing, jostling and talking the sing-song argot of
Glasgow. The clamour of the tramcars, the gleam of the lighted shop
windows in the mud, the clatter of the great Clydesdale dray horses

on the cobblestones and, faintly above, the sound of the ships' sirens coming in on the fog from the nearby Clyde – this was the vivid, vital, unselfconscious teeming life of Glasgow that he was so used to! Then he would board a train that took him away into the Lanarkshire hills, towards the twinkling villages, out into one of those muddy sunsets sinking over the Clyde Estuary, home to darkening Bellshill, Mossend.

Though not born in Glasgow, he shared many of that city's characteristics: its volubility, its enthusiasm, and its swift shifts of mood. Glasgow is said to long to be loved and James certainly longed to be loved. Yet in the east, far from home, he felt spurned: Fifers are known for more than an ordinary share of caution and shrewdness. They looked upon his naive Glaswegian naughtiness with a certain indifference.

His trickery, his finessing were not going to impress here: much more than fireworks was demanded. And yet he could not fathom exactly what was wanted. When expressed in dull tactical terms – 'chase after the man in possession' – it made little sense to him. Puzzled and undoubtedly homesick, James abandoned himself to despair. His confidence and pawky chatterbox charm disintegrated into bewildered, loud-mouthed but ultimately futile defiance:

> I couldn't alter my style. I had been in dead earnest when I told Mr Logan there was nothing for it but packing up. It was a hard knock all the same. I had hoped to make football my career and this seemed the end.

It was at this point that Morrison's influence proved decisive:

> The next morning I was making my way to Stark's Park when whom should I meet but Alec James. Whether this meeting was by accident or design I cannot know, but it was quite evident he had been anxious to see me.
>
> We walked together to Stark's Park and took a seat in the old grandstand. We had a long talk over the events that had taken place.

Morrison had little to offer except to counsel patience and to insist the little man have more faith in himself. James had had his bluff called; and Morrison offered him a way back. According to James, Morrison's talk 'gave me fresh heart and saved me from finishing up'.

And just like in the fairy story, within a few weeks James got another chance. As part of a much-altered Raith side, he played well, the team won, and he was never dropped again while at Raith. Always insisting on having the last word, he wrote some time later: 'Raith Rovers went from strength to strength that season and I heard no more about having to change my game. Wee Alex was left to play the game that suited him best.'

Which may have been less than the truth for, though James was impetuous and argumentative and generally something of a nuisance at times, he was no fool. A comment he made to Morrison just prior to being given his chance to get back into the first team, that 'if I can't play myself then I'll make Jennings, the centre-forward, play' suggests that he was determined to learn from his experience. To be fair to James, he was always going to find it difficult to fit into a new side. From the very outset, it would seem that he demanded the team revolve around *him*, and as Morrison admitted: 'It is not always easy to divine what he is to do with the ball. His play is mystifying to the opposition and also to his own clubmates.'

It is small wonder that the down-to-earth Raith Rovers board were unimpressed by such a phenomenon. Without Morrison's guiding 'vision' they would have seen nothing at this stage but a tiny, cheeky, occasionally brilliant but often totally bemusing player, when they were looking for something much more direct and to the point.

Football had rapidly become a matter of pounds, shillings and pence: a commercial enterprise with very tight profit margins. Success on the field was crucial for solvency and in Scotland, with the major trophies almost exclusively in the hands of the Old Firm season after season, it was hard for a club like Raith Rovers to keep in balance.

But for Morrison, the determination to nurse and cultivate the exotic plant he had chanced upon was not to be thwarted. Perhaps, like Alex's brother Charlie, he saw in James a surrogate son. His own son had caused him some distress: he married a local grocer's daughter, then deserted her upon the birth of their first child, leaving behind him massive debts and scandal. Morrison was clearly devoted to James:

Here was a young boy on the threshold of a great career, a great
player, in my opinion, in the making . . . I wanted to improve him
in every way and urged him to read the best of literature. I invited
him to my house and gave him books to read. Regularly every
Thursday, Alec put in an appearance and left with two books
under his arm to do him until the following week.

Whether James actually read the books is another matter.
Morrison's concern for the boy was certainly known to his parents
– when James was sent off the field in consecutive weeks and
received a two-week's suspension:

It was at this time that his father sent me a letter which I still
possess telling me how grateful he was for all I had done for his
boy, for the fatherly interest I had taken in him and sympathising
with me, well knowing how sore I felt at the unfortunate position
in which Alec found himself at that time.

And Morrison's concern continued well after James had left for
greater things. Almost 50 years after James won his first Cup Final
medal for Arsenal, an old scrap-book was found at the bottom of a
cupboard at Stark's Park, chronicling that great achievement,
packed with cuttings from a score of newspapers and magazines,
pictures, articles and cartoons.
    It had been compiled by Bob Morrison.

6

The 'Lang Toon'

Some say the devil's deid
An' buried in Kirkcaldy . . .   Traditional

THOUGH ALEX JAMES spent only three years in Kirkcaldy, from October 1922 to September 1925, they were years of consolidation where his personal life was concerned. He developed physically, established himself in his profession, he met and married Peggy Willis, started a family, travelled abroad for the first time and, most significantly, he discovered golf.

It has been said that nowhere in the world does the young male take more sweetly and more naturally to golf than in Scotland – and particularly in Fife, where the springy turf, washed and influenced by the grey North Sea provides an ideal natural surface for Scotland's most famous links.

By the 1920s the game was a national pastime and for Fife and Kirkcaldy it was a thriving industry. Since the War the world had gone 'golf-crazy' and, with the game's ever-increasing popularity in America, the demand for equipment was such that a healthy export trade had quickly grown up with Fife clubmakers in the vanguard.

It is perhaps ironic, in the light of subsequent events, that golf and romance came together for Alex James. His falling in love with the game was simultaneous with his falling in love with Peggy Willis, his future wife. She would look back in later years to rue the infuriating but, to its addicts, inescapably alluring game: for Alex became an addict and Peggy a 'golf widow.'

In 1924, however, she was just a girl:

I was only 15. I hadn't been in Kirkcaldy for more than a few weeks, and I had a job in a sports supply shop. The Raith Rovers club would order their kit from the shop, you see. But the man who ran it had been a golf professional, and the shop had once been a photographic studio. At the back there was a large – well, huge – room and in there he would give golf lessons. If you went to him for some golf clubs, he would measure you up – they were made to measure. You had to hit a small fluffy thing at the nets and he would measure your swing. And, before long, he had the greatest hopes for me, that I was going to be the greatest woman golfer ever! What he wasn't going to do! He made me a set of clubs and I had lessons in the shop every day.

By that time I had already met Alec. I had only been in Kirkcaldy for twenty-four hours when I saw him. He's supposed to have said, 'She's for me,' to his pal, George Barton. I was just a kid, mind, wearing black woollen stockings, and I certainly hadn't been impressed by him.

James remembered their meeting some years later:

One day I was in the confectionary shop which Jimmy Logan, our manager, kept at Kirkcaldy. George Barton, our reserve right back, was with me. Suddenly the door opened and Davie Willis, Raith Rover's trainer, walked in with a girl – Peggy, his daughter.

Dave turned to Peggy and said, 'There are two of our players.'

'What, does that little smout play football?' asked Peggy, staring at me incredulously.

I didn't hear this conversation until afterwards and, when I did, I swore I'd make Peggy pay for it. I married her and she's been paying for it ever since.

Their unlikely courtship proceeded in the face of initial hostility from Peggy's father. He had no objection to James personally; it was only that he did not want his daughter to get involved with footballers. In fact, he made efforts to keep her away from them:

There was a theatre in Kirkcaldy called the Opera House. It used to get musicals most of the time and, in between, movies. Footballers were allowed to go there for free on a Monday so Father used to say to me, 'You're not to go there on a Monday night – you can go on a Tuesday.'

I used to sit in the ticket-booth with the lady who sold tickets and then I would get in free, too. But Alec used to go home to Glasgow at the weekends at first, and so he would go to the Theatre on a Tuesday. Dad didn't know this! And that was the start of the romance. He asked me if he could take me home. I was already being walked home by a chap called Charlie Barclay, the local boy with all the money! But Alec wasn't discouraged. He just said, well, next week. And that was the end of Charlie Barclay and the start of Alec James.

Father didn't think much of it at the time, but my mother was on my side. She would pass out sandwiches for Alec to eat when we were standing at the garden gate. She thought he looked as though he didn't get enough to eat. He was no more than eight and a half stone then – and I was nine stone!

I would get tickets to go to the football matches from the man who ran the sports shop where I worked. When he didn't want to go he'd let me off for the afternoon. Alec was remarkable to watch – no one scored goals like he did; for a man so small, he had such powerful little legs . . .

And thus, with a romance developing with the golfing tomboy who lived just along the street, James settled into the little town of Kirkcaldy.

He was a popular young man; according to the son of the Club chairman, Andrew Adamson:

He earned himself quite a reputation as a 'ladies' man' and the dance hostesses at the local Palais were amongst his friends. Within a short time he'd acquired an AJS motorcycle which was forever breaking down and he was always calling on the son of another director, Fraser, who also had a motor-bike, to get him to help fix it.

A team-mate, Alec Cowie, thought the young James a shrewd individual:

He wasn't a boozer, though he liked to have a good time. He was a decent lad, football daft, but not at all loud-mouthed; well-spoken and temperate in his habits. I never knew of him being the worse for drink.

He stayed across the road from me in digs in Barnet Crescent
– it was a new housing development. You got full board, three
meals a day and most of the players who stayed in Kirkcaldy
would be boarded out like that. Alec used to go home to Glasgow
at the weekends, at first, like myself. But once he started with
Peggy he stayed in Kirkcaldy, even during the summer.

In Kirkcaldy, if you were a player with the team, you were
definitely somebody. The directors were all prominent businessmen, proud of their town and of their club. And so were the
people. You could go to all the theatres and cinemas for free –
but, though it was a fair-sized place, it was small in the gossip
sense. Alec would say that his landlady was the local Empire
News; you couldn't move anywhere in Kirkcaldy but that she
would tell you within a day or so exactly where you had been!
But there was little unpleasant scandal – the team were all sensible lads, sober lads – respectable working-class if you like . . .

It is no exaggeration to say that the Raith club was something of a
'family' affair. Many of the directors were involved in more than
just the commercial and industrial life of the town. There was a
strong tradition of local businessmen involving themselves in
education, charity, local politics, and members of the Kirkcaldy
Board certainly took a close interest in the welfare of their players.
Unlike in some small industrial towns, where a place on the board
of the local football team could be bought for a lump sum down,
where the players were treated like chattels and where the directors'
hospitality room was a privileged world apart, at Kirkcaldy
directors felt they had a much more enlightened part to play.

Mr Adamson, the club's chairman, took an active part in local
civic affairs: he was chairman of the Fife Education Committee and
later a town councillor, magistrate and treasurer of the burgh. He
was also prominent in the Scottish Football Association as a selec-
tor and as a linesman for internationals. He often had players up to
his house for an evening meal and Cowie recalled:

I used to go home to Glasgow after a match when I first joined
the club and sometimes there wouldn't be a train, or I'd miss it,
and have to stay over, and Adamson would invite me into the
family pew at church.

Kirkcaldy itself, with its thriving industry, its busy sea-port, and a history stretching back to the days when much of its trade was carried out directly with Holland, had much else besides its football club to be proud of. It boasted among its famous 'sons' Adam Smith, author of the *Wealth of Nations;* Robert Adam, architect and designer for King George III; Sir Sandford Fleming, the inventor of Standard Time; and many more outstanding missionaries, inventors, educators, all of whom reflected the deep and long-standing relationship which Kirkcaldy (and Fife in general) has had with educational, philosophical and scientific advance; St Andrews, just along the coast was, after all, the first university in Great Britain.

Coal-mines and linoleum works were Kirkcaldy's main claim to industrial fame. Situated a mile or so to the north of the town, the linoleum factory chimneys belched black smoke over the town, the strange odour of hot linseed oil from the linoleum-making process giving rise to the famous lines:

> *For I ken masel'*
> *By the queer-like smell*
> *That the next stop's Kirkcaldy.*

However, when James arrived and took up digs in Barnet Crescent he was settling into a district, Linkstown, that was dotted with mainly small-scale industrial works, some still using electricity generated by water-mills. There were engineering works, rope- and cable-makers supplying the nearby ship-building industry; small-scale textile factories, some still, like so many chapels, summoning their workers early each morning with bells hung in turrets. Just behind Stark's Park were clay-pits from which a score of local pottery firms, pipe-makers and glass-works took their raw material, many of the last situated close to the seashore in the alleys or 'wynds' that led from the coast road up to the famous Links Road along which each year ran the country's longest market.

The year of 1922 saw unemployment rising in Kirkcaldy, just as it was all over Scotland. The local paper regularly carried pictures and tales of men of all trades leaving for Canada and the USA. But although there was hardship, the problem did not seem as grim here as in Lanarkshire and Bellshill, because Kirkcaldy was then still a strikingly beautiful little town. A short walk from Stark's Park was the sea front, from where the coast could be seen to curve away to the east, past Kirkcaldy and Dysart, and out into the North Sea.

When the tide was out, off-shore rocks rich in plant and bird-life were revealed, regularly visited by seals and curlews. When foggy, the fog-horns from ships and lighthouses sounded ghostly, a score of lights flashed, while on clear days the Pentland Hills across the Firth of Forth could be glimpsed.

We can be sure Alex James wasted little time gazing over the Firth at seals, nor contemplating the history of the famous sons of Kirkcaldy (although the fact that Scotland's last King Alexander, Alexander III, toppled over the cliffs at nearby Kinghorn in 1286 may have amused him). The sea, in fact, held little attraction for him. Yet it was from Kirkcaldy that James would set off for his first trip abroad – one that simply confirmed in him his dislike of travel in general . . .

The Raith Rovers party – a mere 13 players (including one just recovering from an operation) plus manager and directors – set off for the Canary Isles in May 1923. It seemed they were more in search of sun and fun than strenuous opposition, with a stop off at Vigo in Spain to watch a bullfight as part of the itinerary. Indeed, the trip might have remained no more than a footnote in the club's history had the ship carrying the team not run aground on the rocks off the Spanish coast.

Alec Cowie, one of the party, recalled the moment of impact:

> We had set out on a Saturday morning and the next day I was up early on deck. It was my first time at sea, and I saw a man a little way off in a boat, standing and waving his arms – couldn't hear what he was calling. I didn't know what to do, but just then a member of the crew came up with a bucket of rubbish to throw overboard. And I thought, well, he'll report it. So I went back down to my cabin. It was seven in the morning and there was a sudden bump!
>
> We were all ordered on deck with out lifebelts. I grabbed my purse and went up, just wearing sandshoes. When I got on deck everything seemed so peaceful I was tempted to go back down to my cabin for my walking shoes, but the sight of a small pool of water in the corridor made my mind up!

Tom Jennings remembered the impact as a 'tremendous smash!'

Alex James remembered nothing at all, claiming that he was having a bath at the time:

> Someone was banging away at the door. 'Come on deck, quick. The ship's sinking!' I thought it was all a kid. One or other of them was always trying to get a laugh out of me so I shouted back that I was coming and went on with my bath. But slowly it dawned on me that there must be something wrong. Whistles were being blown on deck. I could hear folk running about and shouting.

The grounding of the ship had been a deliberate act by the captain, who had seen the rocks and decided not to risk veering away in case he gashed the side of the boat open. When the tide turned, he calculated, the boat would float off with no harm done . . . But serious damage had been sustained, and all crew and passengers were forced to evacuate.

For Alex James, this first impression of foreign soil did not impress him:

> I suppose it would be about 10 o'clock in the morning when we were landed on an island, the name of which I could never remember. I've always called it Cannibal Island for few of the fishermen on it seemed hardly civilised. They had absolutely nothing to give us except two or three loaves of bread. Those women who got the ration wished they hadn't, for it was sour.

In later recollections, he would refer to 'breadfruit', gold sovereigns and even missionaries – thus conveniently confusing whole hemispheres, not to mention civilisations.

The island was, in fact, Villa Garcia, a small fishing village in the Galicia region of north-west Spain – remote and harsh terrain perhaps, but no tropical jungle. Their original destination, Vigo, a mile down the coast where they had intended to watch the bullfight could not be reached in time; after a meal in a local village they returned to the ship to spend the night.

The next day the party was taken to Vigo to spend the night.

> We got there to find a meal and beds awaiting us. I don't know which was the worst. The food was cooked in olive oil and I

couldn't fancy it. While the beds – I'd have sooner slept in a 'model'. At darkness I tried my best to get some sleep but it was no good.

But it was a stable, more or less. We had the upstairs part – the children had presumably been ousted. We went up the stairs but it was one of those rooms with a hole in the middle of the floor, with a barnyard and animals just below. We took one look and left and slept on the seats of the bus!

All of which may seem strange when one remembers the sleeping conditions back home in the tenement houses of Glasgow and Bellshill where many of the players hailed from: damp walls, bed-bugs and half a dozen bodies to a bed . . .

The ship having been refloated and the baggage unloaded, the weary and culture-shocked passengers were taken from Vigo on to Lisbon and the Canaries by a passing P and O liner for the rest of their relatively uneventful tour.

Though they played at least five games, including one against Scottish Third Lanark who were calling in on their way back from a much more ambitious trip to South America, Alex James was soon bored.

What had started out as a merry romp in glorious weather with the little man settling down for 'a rattling good time with deck-games and practical jokes' with his pals ('practical jape-mongers all of them . . . I could write for days of the many original pranks we played . . .') had rapidly palled. He had soon run out of cash:

I found I had to hand out tips pretty freely as we went along and, excepting experience, I couldn't see the tour being profitable. That is what footballers always discover when they go abroad. The money just runs away in odds and ends . . . the football wasn't football and against the vigorous defenders I had to look mighty slippy to escape without more than bruises. We remained there a fortnight and I was glad when the time came to come home again . . . After a couple of days in Las Palmas I didn't know what on earth to do with myself . . .

James's foreign trips would, in future, be infrequent and often on the bizarre side. He was a poor traveller, especially by air and sea;

even the ferry trip across to Belfast for an international match filled him with dread.

In fact, there would only be one foreign journey that would appeal to him in the coming seasons – the crossing of the border into England. And it was not long before he was being tempted by a variety of destinations.

7

The Famous Five

In Kirkcaldy, as in all parts of Fife, the sparrows are said to fly with their tails to the wind to keep the dirt out of their eyes. Some folks have been trying to throw 'stoor' in the eyes of the Raith Rovers directors by spinning tales of £50,000 bids for their forward line. Some dust!

Sunday Mail, November 1925

JAMES'S FOOTBALL CAREER had begun in earnest. The Raith side were, as he put it, 'a happy crowd' and Stark's Park was the perfect little stage upon which he could perform and learn.

He had joined the club at a critical point in its short history. Founded in 1883, it had moved to Stark's Park, at the southern end of Kirkcaldy and overlooking the Firth of Forth in the Linkstown district, in 1890.

The club had entered the Second Division in 1902, had won the championship twice before gaining entry (this before the days of automatic promotion and relegation) to the First Division in 1911. In 1913 it reached the Scottish Cup Final. The War had intervened but now, ten years on from that great Cup Final day, much was expected. These were heady days, when big success appeared a possibility to supporters who had seen the team finish third to the Old Firm, Rangers and Celtic, in 1922 – its best-yet achievement in the League.

The 1921/22 team had been a well-balanced one with formidable half-backs: Raeburn, Morris and Collier, the latter two Scottish internationals. With solid full backs, a secure and experienced goalkeeper and a fine forward line with the Duncan brothers on the right wing, a free-scoring young centre-forward in Tom Jennings and speed on the left wing with Bobby Archibald, this young exciting team had been on top of the First Division in January 1922. That they had finished in third place was considered no disgrace.

But 1922/23 saw the inevitable stresses and strains occur when a small club with a limited financial base tries to take on the might of established giants growing bigger all the time.

Raith's new grandstand – symbol of hope – was one side of the equation. The simultaneous sale to Leicester City of the two talented Duncan brothers to pay for it was the other. With their departure in July 1922, much of the forward inspiration of the team went too.

When James arrived, Raith Rovers were struggling to keep the momentum of the previous season going; by the time he had secured his place, the 1922/23 season was almost over.

The following season, however, against all odds, the team discovered a new pattern of play, and soon Rovers were mounting a challenge for the title. But it was, in truth, only a minor challenge. By Christmas, Raith – in fourth place – were 10 points adrift of Rangers and January saw them falling further behind. Easter saw Raith register wins over both Rangers and Celtic, James supplying the winning goals, but at season's end his team was still in fourth place, a full 16 points behind Rangers.

The season had been Hughie Gallacher's. Airdrie, his new team, had won the Scottish Cup, Gallacher had topped the scoring chart, and in March he had made his debut for Scotland in a team that included Raith Rovers' Dave Morris.

But if Gallacher was the toast of Scotland, there was no doubting who had emerged as the darling of Stark's Park. For a time, it had seemed that the faults of the previous season had not been rectified and in September, Raith was defeated 2-1 by Queens Park: the *Kirkcaldy Times* was drawn to criticise: 'James was displaying his old tendency to selfishness and many good chances were lost because he kept the ball instead of parting with it to his mates.'

In mid-October another Raith defeat (4-0 by Hibernians) was also attributed by the *Kirkcaldy Times* to James's 'dillying and dallying', but the following week, when Raith beat Third Lanark 6-1, James appeared to have heeded the correspondent's advice: 'There was none of the over-dedication to trickery which has so spoiled his play recently.'

A week later, he scored what even the *Kirkcaldy Times* reporter considered

one of the most spectacular goals seen at Stark's Park for many a day. Twists and turns left four defenders absolutely dazzled and

landed James in front of Nisbet (the goalkeeper) with the ball at
his feet. The pair eyed one another for a second or more and
directly Nisbet made a move, the Raith man walked the ball into
the net, leaving the goalie to wonder how it had been done . . .

This crescendo of praise and achievement peaked rather unex-
pectedly in November when James was sent off twice, on consecutive Saturdays and one can understand why James might have
attracted rough play at times when listening to Tom Jennings'
account of one of the incidents:

Wee Alec used to put the ball over his head and back heel it over
again. This time he did it twice with Tom Scott standing waiting
for him. As the back moved in, the wee fellow hooked the ball
over his head when he was passing. Tom said, 'No you don't.'
There was a bit of a scuffle and Alec James was ordered off. Scott
soon followed . . .

For the remainder of the season he rarely drew a critical word, and
by season's end, he had made something of a name for himself.

James's football progress at Kirkcaldy had been quite remarkable. On arrival at Stark's Park in 1922 he had found life hard and
had impressed only Bob Morrison. Yet, by March 1924, he was
being discussed in the Scottish press as a potential international,
one of three possible challengers to Scotland's incumbent inside
left, Tommy Cairns of Rangers.

Indeed, in March 1925 he was selected for a Scottish international trial at Tynecastle where he played alongside Hughie
Gallacher and Willie Russell in the 'B' side.

In terms of physique, he had hardly changed at all since his 'Cannibal' days – no taller, perhaps half a stone heavier, but he now had
the ability to extract great power from those short, sturdy legs.
Trainer Dave Willis must take a great deal of the credit for gradually
building James up; in the very early days he put Alex on a diet of
cod-liver oil to be taken each evening. And training, in those far-off
days, placed a great deal of emphasis on stamina and leg-work.
Willis recalled:

When I first went to Kirkcaldy I may as well admit it I was far from popular. I came as a new broom determined to sweep clean. The players later admitted that they felt ever so fit for my methods, but at first I was put down as a 'slave driver'.

Willis placed great stress on vigorous walking. Alec Cowie recalled that it was rare that training was conducted with a football:

> The trainers worked on the principle that the less you saw of the ball during the week the more eager you would be to get hold of it on match day! So we rarely saw a ball during training. Maybe on a Wednesday there would be some five-a-side, but for the rest it was roadwork. We would go to a village a few miles out and walk back into town – fast.

James also recalled those route marches:

> I reported at Stark's Park for training. Dave Willis introduced me to the boys, who were going for a stiff walk. Davie was really kind-hearted. He looked me over just before the start.
>
> 'We're away,' he said kindly. 'Just you follow at your leisure.' And away they set off at a great pace, leaving the wee fellow to follow quietly behind. He wasn't to be overstrained.
>
> Later some of the boys, keeping up the joke of telling me to 'walk at my own pace', suggested I was left behind as they liked the townsfolk to know they were footballers in training. With me amongst them it would look more like a boy's outing.
>
> Soon after we went to Portobello to take Turkish baths.
>
> 'Let's see you on the scales, Alec,' some bright wit called out. Eight stone four pounds. What a laugh! The lightest player in professional football. And all I could offer in excuse was that I had a good pair of legs. That was about all. They must have had many a quiet laugh at wee Alec in those days but I found them real good pals on and off the field.

Despite his size, his shooting powers startled both his team-mates and those seeing him from the terraces of Stark's Park for the first time. Newspaper reports were studded with references to 'rocket-shots' and goalkeepers being 'rooted to the spot'. He admitted to having practised assiduously – and with a football!

I used to go out all afternoon practising taking the ball whichever way it came to me. Dave Morris sent it to me from all angles and at all heights. I hit it first time until by practice I was a pretty deadly shot and could boot the ball accurately without losing time bringing it under control.

It was not so much brute force, however, as timing:

> I had two good feet and had mastered the art of correct timing. And the mastery of the art has been very useful to me as a wee player . . . quick surprise shooting, shooting without stopping – the secret of the success lies in that . . .

'Where little James gets all the beef which he puts into his shots, I, for one, do not know,' wrote the correspondent of the *Kirkcaldy Times* in April 1924.

In his first season or so there had been constant references to his tendency to hold the ball too long, to overdo the 'tricks' – ironic, coming from Scottish observers, Scotland being the land of the ball-player. But while it was true that he often looked lost in a world of his own, twisting, wriggling his way around the field in the fashion of his great hero Patsy Gallacher, yet when such tactics came off, as they increasingly began to do, they made the game appear magical: defenders beaten by the suggestion of a turn, or sent sprawling by a side-step, a sudden change of direction, a movement of the foot over the ball to suggest one thing, the ball itself travelling somewhere else entirely.

Such methods were often strongly criticised, particularly in the local press, but if the so-called experts found fault, the crowds were soon flocking to see James. All eyes would focus on him – he was 'cleverness personified', or a 'bag-of-tricks at all times and highly amusing'. And with the crowds enthralled, it was not long before the scouts were watching closely too.

Just before the James double dismissal, there had been much press ballyhoo over a reputed £50,000 bid by Millwall (then in England's Third Division) for the entire Raith forward line.

An offhand remark-cum-joke to a reporter in the Banks Restaurant in Glasgow by a Raith director about being willing to sell all five men had been seized upon, much to everyone's amusement, and blown up out of all proportion. Ludicrous though the offer was, it highlighted the uncomfortable fact that, despite all the hopes and dreams of the Raith supporters, a club such as Raith was no more than a shop-window. The players could just as well have run out on to the pitch with price tags round their necks.

Alec Cowie, training to be a schoolmaster while waiting his chance to break into Raith's first team, had ample time to observe the Raith team at close quarters and considered none of them to be 'mercenaries':

> They were a decent bunch of lads, not a roughneck or a hooligan among them. They were all good players, you see, and you need some intelligence to be a good player. They weren't young boys, either – most had trades, though only a few of them carried on with their jobs as far as I recall.
>
> Brown, the keeper, was a painter and decorator. He lived in Glasgow and travelled to Raith for home games, as did Bobby Archibald. I don't know what his trade was but he was forever bringing in bargains of some kind that he would try to sell us all – shirts and whatnot . . .
>
> Miller was a civil servant in Edinburgh and Raeburn was a joiner with the Water Company, so they would have to have time off to play. Bill Collier had been a miner and Morris had been a shipyard worker – most of them had similar trades.
>
> We were all on good wages. It was £6 a week at that time, with £2 a win and £1 a draw. And £4 a week all through the summer. That was standard, though some men earned a bit more according to their contract. But even for me, earning £3.10s in the 'A' team and £4 a week as a teacher, it was very good money. I only trained on a Tuesday and a Thursday and the First team didn't do a lot more . . .

And yet ambition still tugged away at many of the Raith players. At 1923/24 season's end, Inglis and Collier, having resisted the blandishments of American scouts recruiting for a new US Football League, went to Sheffield Wednesday, closely followed by goalkeeper Brown, who went to local club Dunfermline. Bobby Archibald went to Third Lanark and thence to Stoke City. Within a few months of the 1924/25 season starting Tom Jennings had gone to Leeds for £3,000; Miller had already moved on to Hearts. And all the while there were reports of scouts and managers and agents moving across the Kindgom of Fife like so many locusts.

No wonder that, by the end of the 1924/25 season, Raith had managed to achieve no better than ninth position. And, inevitably, it was announced in the *Kirkcaldy Times*: 'James, of Raith Rovers, who showed exceptional shooting powers at Hampden, can be had by any club willing to fork up "the doings". The Kirkcaldy club are prepared to transfer him if the cheque speaks loudly enough . . .'

James himself, however, was involved in none of the early negotiations with clubs such as Liverpool, Aston Villa, Huddersfield and Leicester City. He was as much at mercy of the newspaper headlines as the man in the street:

In Kirkcaldy there are no such things as football secrets. Consequently I knew all about it every time people came north to sound the Rovers directors regarding my transfer. Sometimes the postman put me wise. Sometimes it was the telegraph boy.

However, when he heard that Newcastle United was interested in signing him he grew excited:

I thought I was going to land there and I was really pleased. Davie Willis, my father-in-law, was an old Newcastle United player and very enthusiastic for the club, and one way and another I set my heart on getting there.

The weeks passed by and the rumours tailed off. Negotiations between the clubs – if ever there were any – must have ended. I heard no more of Newcastle.

James found the 1925/26 season starting, and the sense of anti-climax after all the false transfer trails prompted an initial skirmish with Raith Rovers when signing-on time came along. 'I had a bit of a dispute with Rovers over terms and started the season by refusing to play in the first team on the grounds that I was unfit.'

There was disruption and dissension in the air – something that would in future years become something of a commonplace where James was concerned. It was reported at the time that both the club doctor and trainer had pronounced him fit but that it was clear he was in no mood to play. Rumour now had it that he was angling for a transfer to Nottingham Forest, the club to which trainer and father-in-law Willis had just gone.

Late in 1924 James had finally married Peggy Willis at a small ceremony in Edinburgh. There had been no honeymoon; their daughter Patsy said:

> Mum remembers she bought a new hat for the occasion but that the whole thing wasn't very romantic. She came home on the wedding night, she said, to Alec's digs in Barnet Crescent to find she had to cook supper for him and the other player lodging there at the time. Dad hadn't told her about him, and all she had was a little gas-ring.

Within a short time they had moved down the street to live with Peggy's parents, but they made no attempt to get a house of their own as for most of the season it had been clear that James would be moving to another club. The only question had been where:

> The wedding was a hurried affair: neither Alec's parents was there, though by now his mother was getting on and was confined to a wheel-chair. She died soon afterwards. Mum said that the first thing they bought was a phonograph, but they could only get one record to play on it – Ave Maria. They played that over and over . . .

In July 1925 Alec James Junior was born and with Peggy's parents packing up to move to Nottingham, and Alec still not sure of his eventual destination, it was an unsettling period for Peggy. Alec, however, appeared to be taking things very much in his stride:

> It was the Edinburgh autumn holiday and I was keen to see the two great games being staged there: Hibernian versus Celtic in the morning and Hearts versus Rangers in the afternoon.
>
> I had just got to the station at Kirkcaldy when a fellow I scarcely knew asked me if it was right that I was 'booked' for Preston. He had just got it from a friend who had been told by his cousin, etc.
>
> 'Och, it's just talk,' I said, making for my train.
>
> I never gave it a second thought, for I didn't want to be bothered on a holiday with those kinds of rumours. I'd heard quite enough of them. I met a whole host of football pals at Edinburgh but none of them mentioned Preston to me.
>
> After the Hearts game I had no fancy for hurrying back to

Kirkcaldy and went along to see a show at one of the city's theatres.

I caught the last train home from Edinburgh. It was midnight when I stepped on the platform at Kirkcaldy and the first person I saw – there weren't many around! – was Jim Logan.

He bustled up. 'Alec,' he said, 'the Preston people are up to fix your transfer. I want you to come along to the hotel to talk things over.'

James Taylor, director of Preston and the driving force behind the famous old Lancashire club, had developed an interest in James towards the end of the 1924/25 season and had been pestering manager Jimmy Logan for many months; he had made at least three visits to Scotland to watch James.

The weekend of the signing had seen a breakthrough on Saturday morning. Logan had told Taylor that Adamson had decided to open negotiations. Taylor, then in Kirkcaldy, wired the Preston directorate to assemble on Sunday morning:

I raced back to Preston through the night in order to get there in time for the meeting and persuaded the board to grant me £3,000 with which to buy James. (The club had originally only assigned £2,500.) As soon as the deal was fixed I left with two of my colleagues by car for Scotland again.

One of the colleagues, Captain Billy Sharples, recalled the occasion years later – remembering the excitement of the chase as they travelled in his open car across the snow-strewn Scotland. And thus the motor car demonstrated its increasing influence and significance in the affairs of men.

The drama did not stop there, though. Within a day, James was to be whisked off to make his debut in a mid-week match at Middlesbrough, but not before he had experienced some twinges of doubt and regret, however:

Now, here's a funny thing about that transfer. It wasn't until the next morning that I began to think about what was going to happen to me when I arrived at Deepdale. Then it dawned on me that North End had four first-class inside lefts: Frank Jeffries, Ronnie Woodhouse, Horace Barnes and George Sapsford.

Raith Rovers in their hotel headquarters during their trip to the Canary Islands,
Standing; Brown; seated left to right; Ritchie, Bell, James, Morris, Cowie and a visitor

1926; James, by now playing for Preston
North End, wearing his first Scottish
cap and the team shirt

With son Alex and daughter Patsy, shortly
before James signed for Arsenal

Alex James, star Arsenal player, with his wife Peggy and their two children
outside their Barnet home in 1934

How the deuce am I ever going to get a game in that team, I kept asking myself. I was dead serious about it. I've always had plenty of confidence in myself but honestly I couldn't see where there was room for Alex James at Deepdale. I wondered if I had made a big blunder in signing without thinking the matter over from every angle.

When I saw the Preston people the next morning I didn't like to put the question to them. I was told, though, that I would be played as soon as possible.

Which was something of an understatement. To get to Middlesbrough on time for the following Wednesday's match meant yet more car dashes. James Taylor appeared to have developed a taste for such adventures:

We couldn't leave Kirkcaldy until the Wednesday morning. The only way to get to Ayresome Park in time was to train it to Edinburgh, motor through to Newcastle and train it again for the last stage to Middlesbrough. [The car journey was enlivened by a leaking radiator] . . . and in those days, garages up there were as scarce as duck-ponds in the Sahara. We had to stop at every farmhouse and ask for a bucket of water to fill the thing up.

Arriving in such undignified haste and suddenly inserted into a team he knew nothing about, it is not surprising that the result was a 5-1 defeat. James played poorly. 'Bad luck has always come to me as soon as I have joined a club.'

And so, Alex James entered English football – bundled unceremoniously over the border in a fast car.

It was the moment that Bob Morrison had dreaded. Saddened and disillusioned by the transfer, he would tender his resignation to the Raith Rovers board:

Mr Morrison came down to the station to see me off to Edinburgh. I was sorry to have to leave behind such a great friend but it had to come sooner or later.

He didn't blame me in the least for going, once the Raith Rovers had been persuaded to part with me. He wished me the best of luck in the future and I recall his parting words on that occasion: 'I'll see you at Wembley!'

8

A Scots Professor

A SEASON OF SHOCKS
Frenzied Search For Players
What 'New Football' has done for the Game.
Seasons of stress and turmoil are nothing new in league football of course but one questions whether in the history of football and its sensations there has ever been a season quite like the present one, with its astounding upheavals on the field of play and its amazing activities behind the scenes.
Topical Times, November 1925

THE YEAR 1925 was a significant one in the history of British football. In March, Dixie Dean – the man who would come to epitomize the English game's massive strengths and ominous weaknesses – made his first-team debut for Everton.

In April, Herbert Chapman bought Alex Jackson, Aberdeen's flying winger, for Huddersfield Town as the latter completed the second in what was to be a record triple championship-winning sequence. In May, however, Chapman suddenly left Huddersfield to become manager of Arsenal – and within a month he had bought Charles Buchan, the first in a long line of expensive stars to make their way to Highbury, helping shift the balance of football power from north to south.

And in June 1925, at a FIFA meeting in Paris, the offside law, that frustrating and, to some, baffling regulation, was altered. The change in the offside law can be stated simply: before the change, if a player did not have at least three opponents between himself and the goal then he was offside; after the change, the number was reduced to two, thus tilting the balance in favour of the attackers.

The idea behind the rule change was that, with the new offside law, more goals would be scored. More goals would mean more excitement and thus more spectators. Club directors had been worried for a year or more about the decline in revenue at the gates. Five years on from the Great War, the initial 'boom' had passed as rival entertainments began to compete for people's time and money. Add to that the economic slump which had impoverished a vast proportion of soccer's traditional audience, and one concludes that a slump in revenues was inevitable. But there was another factor. With more money at stake after the War, the larger League structure by its very nature encouraged a trend towards fast, no-nonsense football designed to ensure 'survival', to avoid the catastrophe of relegation, to cope with the relentless demands of a 42-game (plus Cup matches) eight-month season. There was an ever-increasing impatience with 'fancy' football, or 'slow' play – a desire for speed, speed and more speed. This was coupled with a more defensive frame of mind in the context of which the offside law was crucial. Certain teams perfected 'springing the trap'; games became broken up, stoppages increased – boredom followed.

The underlying causes of soccer's commercial problems were thus economic, social and even psychological. Soccer legislators might have been able to tackle the last by changing their outlook, shifting the emphasis of professional football away from ever-increasing growth and ever more cutthroat competition. But that might have meant sacrificing cash and prestige.

Instead, they tinkered with the rules and simply accelerated the underlying trends; there was, it is true, an initial avalanche of goals and much defensive confusion in the wake of the offside law change. But within a few years, the built-in imperatives of League football ensured that defences once again dominated. Statistics show that the numbers of goals scored declined steadily after 1928, while the pace at which the game was played became quicker and quicker. This apparent mayhem on the field was more than matched by – and no doubt caused – a frenzy off it in the transfer market:

Not a day passes, almost, but one reads of transfers, players with great names moving on; players with names to make are being signed with hearts full of hope. Some clubs keep on getting new men, paying expensive fees . . . I should imagine there's hardly a club in the League which is not joining in the wild chase for new blood and talent to help in the building of winning teams. The competition for men is tremendous and clubs cannot afford to dally.

The most remarkable feature of this spending spree was the

FORTY YEARS OF BOXING BY J. H. LAMBERT SEE INSIDE

TOPICAL TIMES

NO. 316. [REGISTERED AS A NEWSPAPER AT G.P.O.] WEEK ENDING OCTOBER 31, 1925. PRICE 2ᴰ

His First "Cap"

Trickster, tactician, and sharpshooter, Alec James has played superb football since he joined Preston North End from Raith Rovers. His selection as Scotland's inside left against Wales is his first international honour, and it should not be his last.

number of Scottish players entering English football.

In December 1925 *Athletic News* ran an article summing up the year under the headline: 'Gold, Goals and 1925 – Who Wins?' And the fourteen photos of prominent Scots stretching across the top of two pages left one in no doubt as to the answer: Hughie Ferguson, Hughie Gallacher, Dave Morris, Alex James, Willie McStay, Jimmy Gibson, and eight others. 'Never in the history of the game have so many talented Scotsmen been persuaded to make a change. Never have the coffers of Scottish clubs been so lavishly enriched.'

It was the quality of the players being bought that hit the headlines: 'The cream of Scottish football is being skimmed. These are no worn-out warriors that are coming into English play . . .'

As a startling example, the Scottish eleven picked to meet England in April 1925 was one of the few All-Tartan teams, with every player selected being based in Scotland. Eight months later, in December 1925, six of the team had been bought by English clubs and a seventh, Jimmy McMullen, followed soon. Of the four remaining players, significantly, three were Rangers players – Cairns, Meikljohn and Morton and the fourth was a Celtic player. Three years later, the Wembley Wizards, possibly the greatest-ever Scots eleven, included only three players based in Scotland.

But why, one may be tempted to ask, was there such a demand for Scottish players? The Scots might answer – because they were the best. There is some truth in that, but a more compelling reason might be that so many Scots players were available. English clubs with talented players on their books were loath to sell unless they were in the lower divisions, when they were often forced to, just as Scots clubs were. But in Scotland, the imperative to sell was strong even in the First Division: *all* clubs needed the cash, even if they were in the top three or four of the First Division, as Raith had been, as Airdrieonians had been.

The idea that Scots players were somehow more 'artistic', more 'entertaining' because of their traditional ball-playing expertise, had, like most myths, a basis in truth. Scottish League football was less of a treadmill than the English League; with fewer games to play and much less at stake, it was played at a slower pace. Thus, the finer skills and arts of the game could be developed in a somewhat kindlier environment.

The English game was certainly faster, cruder and more concerned with spills and thrills and thus it afforded youngsters less of a chance to put their foot on the ball, as it were, and look up.

The truth was however that Scottish players could, if chosen carefully, provide an English manager with the best of both worlds – a player capable of utilising polished skills in a game no longer designed to develop such skills. That was something Herbert Chapman, Arsenal's new manager, would always understand, and why he rarely bought Scottish players unless they appeared to fit into a tightly organised scheme of things.

By contrast, James Taylor, of Preston North End, was attempting to resurrect that legendary old club by gambling on an almost exclusively Scottish-style team. He could not, perhaps, be blamed, because it had been a similar Scottish influence that had helped establish Preston as one of the great League names back in the very first year of League football in 1889.

In that year, Proud Preston, the Invincibles, had achieved football immortality by winning both the Cup and the League in the same season and, in doing so, had fired Taylor's imagination. He had been a 14-year-old boy standing in the crowd welcoming the heroes back home with the FA Cup. 'I wasn't all that interested in the game,' he told a close friend, 'certainly not passionate about it, although proud of Preston North End as all the lads were at the time; but on that memorable day I was bitten by the football bug, badly bitten, and I have never been able to get it out of my system.'

Taylor had been a director of the club since the War and, apart from a short period between 1921 and 1924 when he had left the board after differences on policy with the shareholders association, he was to continue in office until 1950 when he was made Life President. A wealthy businessman in the pottery trade, he made Preston North End his life: 'He put North End before everything: the League, his home life, even his business. The club he treated like a fond if sometimes troublesome son, thriving to maturity . . .'

Herbert Chapman described Taylor as the 'highest unpaid manager in the game' but he was more powerful than any manager. In the interwar period, managers were still an evolving species. Instead, Taylor worked through others, and much of what 'modern' Preston became can be traced to him. In 1934 they were promoted; in 1937 they were at Wembley only to be beaten by Sunderland. ('He was crying, shedding big tears of disappointment.') But the following year, they returned to win the Cup and almost to take the League as well – the elusive Double!

In 1925, however, Taylor had returned from the wilderness and was setting about raising the club from the state of gloom and debt into which it had sunk after relegation.

Alex James had been just one of seven Scots signed in a burst of spending designed to reawaken interest and bring the crowds flocking back to Deepdale. Taylor's penchant for Scottish players was a source of amusement: 'It was a standing joke that every express train from Scotland brought another man for North End.'

It really was a remarkable fixation. At the start of 1926 out of 30 professionals on the books, 10 were Scots and all were senior first-team players. Sometimes, there would be as many as eight Scots in the side and they rarely came cheaply. The 'school of '25', however, broke all records for spending – almost topping £13,000 in all: apart from James, there was D. Gibson from Kilmarnock; Tom Gillespie from Hearts; Walter Jackson, Alex's brother, from Aberdeen; Willie Russell from Airdrie; while Dave Morris had come from Raith costing £4,700.

It must not be assumed that Taylor's policy was universally popular at the club. At shareholder's meetings his trips north were rediculed and the policy of neighbouring clubs such as Blackpool and Burnley, of discovering and nurturing local talent, was recommended as a cheaper alternative. 'After an outlay of something like £80,000 spent . . . since the war we still have not got a "team", and the name of Preston is a joke ever enjoyed in Scottish football circles . . .' grumbled someone under the headline, 'Preston Supporter Hits Out' *Thomson's Weekly News* of March 1929.

As a consequence, however, James entered a side that contained no budding youngsters and, though much money had been spent, it would emerge that he was the only valuable man on the staff – someone whom the club could hope to sell again for a substantial fee.

Willie Russell, for instance, had cost more than James but would prove to have played his best football for Airdrieonians where, alongside Hughie Gallacher, he had helped win the club the Scottish Cup in 1924 as well as given Rangers a good run for their money in the League. He had won caps for Scotland in 1924 and 1925 but after joining Preston he would be selected no more. After 1925/6, when he made 40 appearances scoring 12 goals, he was switched to half-back but, by 1928, he was no longer a regular in the side. After a further 29 appearances over three seasons he was given a free transfer in 1931.

Preston would be challengers for the Second Division title for two consecutive seasons while James was with them, so as a team they could obviously play reasonable football at times. But they flattered to deceive. James quickly became the hub of the side and if, through injury or international calls, the team had to do without him, they were revealed as bereft of imagination and class. In trawling so widely, Taylor had certainly discovered the much sought-after 'pearl', but his ultimate departure would reveal the barrenness of his first attempt to restore Preston's pride.

The strength of the Preston side during James's warly days at Deepdale was the defence. In a period of tactical confusion and mayhem with goals being scored in hundreds up and down the country, Preston North End, marshalled around Dave Morris – the other Scot who had cost more than James – were able to restrict the goal rush, conceding just 52 goals in 1926/27 while Blackburn, Burnley and Blackpool were letting in 80, 96 and 80 respectively.

What Preston lacked, and had done for years before James's arrival, was a forward line that could score consistently and heavily. Even Blackpool, Preston's unpretentious neighbours and Second Division colleagues, could boast of forwards like local boy Beel who regularly notched up 30 goals a season for the seasiders (scoring 120 over six seasons) and, later, the great Jimmy Hampson, whose goals would take Blackpool into the First Division in 1930 – much to Preston's chagrin. In September 1926, however, Preston set out with high hopes and after eight games played they were second in the League; in October 'Perseus' in the *Lancashire Daily Post* under the headline 'What Alex James Stands For: A Dribbling Object Lesson', took a closer look at Preston's new and unusual man. 'Perseus' felt James was swimming against a prevailing tide of stereotyped moves and mass-produced football. James was:

a man who is not afraid to depart from the ruck to cultivate arts that most of his contemporaries have never dreamt of, to dribble and to demonstrate to a generation which is satisfied with fustian what the real cloth of the game is made of . . .

However, James was also part of a modern 'system'; one that was not working. By December, with results beginning to go against them, a letter-writing campaign to the local press began:
'I thought James was an inside forward. He's not. He's a half-

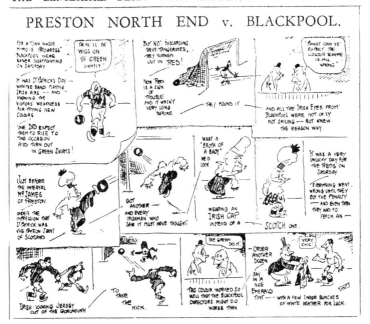

back!' wrote one. 'Why do these men', wrote another, referring to both James and Russell, 'continue to adopt this semi-half-back position instead of keeping up the field along with the centre-forward and wing-men? Surely our half-backs are strong enough to cope with anything in the Second Division? By hanging back they hinder not help the defence . . .'

There had been protests the preceding season when Preston had first unveiled their 'W' formation – the standard response to the new offside law. With the increasing freedom afforded the centre-forward, defences were left little alternative but to restrict the forward movement of the centre-half who now stayed close to his full backs and thus no longer played a full part in attack, once the principal function of a centre-half. But there were other changes occurring, too:

A LOOSE HEAD IN FOOTBALL: A NEW GAME WHICH MOST OF THE INSIDE WING MEN ARE NOW PLAYING
The inside wing men no longer play the part in football that they

used to play. Instead of going up to do their one-time share in the attack they are almost without exception inclined to hang back so that in the first place they are able to fill the gap which is now left by the centre-half becoming a sort of third full back and in the second place they are the men who feed the other forwards.

Topical Times, 1925

These changes had been occurring gradually ever since the War but the offside law change had hastened them along and, in a sense, had allowed the audience less time in which to adjust. It had not been so long ago that inside forwards had been the goal-scorers with the centre-forward acting as linkman, spraying passes to the wings or holding it before slipping passes through for the inside men to run on to. Now it was centre-forwards who were scoring, aided by wingers; to some on the terraces it must have seemed that the world was turning upside down.

Indeed, the reactions of the crowds were as interesting as the changes themselves – an early example of 'consumer resistance'. *Topical Times* had reported: 'It is a fact that the supporters of Blackburn Rovers have more than once expressed their disapproval of Puddefoot's method in keeping well to the rear of the other forwards . . .' while in Preston on the terraces, the abuse and cat-calling and barracking made commentators like 'Perseus' uneasy:

'The method the team is adopting is making the crowd very impatient and there is an ugly note creeping into the attitude towards the players.' Tolerance was called for. There had already been trouble on the terraces when clinkers had been thrown at the opposing team, leading to notices being posted around the ground threatening FA action. Could it be that the crowd might start attacking their own men?

That both James and centre-half Morris continued to score goals during their period at Preston is evidence that the despised W-formation was not adhered to exclusively. Indeed, part of the crowd's frustration was due to the fact that James could and did score spectacular goals and it seemed to them such a waste not to have him up there on the edge of the opponents penalty area potting at goal. That he did score goals was also evidence that the W-system could prove deficient if the side employing it did not possess wingers capable of cutting inside and acting as inside forwards when the occasion demanded.

Harrison, James's outside left, was a winger of an earlier era who had begun his career with Everton before the First World War; add to that the fact that, for a season or two, Preston was bedevilled with the problem of having no one of quality on the right wing and it is clear that James was often forced to go forward on occasions and take on the responsibility for scoring as well as creating. His task was, as a consequence, an onerous one.

Surveying the 1926/27 season at its end, in May 1927, when Preston had missed promotion by just a few points, 'Perseus' commented:

Tom Roberts, who is leading Preston North End's attack with characteristic verve.

The attack became in essence an attack of two men: James and Roberts, with the former as initiator and prompter and the latter to drive the movements home. James, as ever, came in for a lot of criticism from the superficial observer because he attempted too much and because he fetched the ball too much and didn't go through with it but what the line was without him was disclosed

by the happenings in the last few weeks. Far too much depended
on the efforts of the inside left and the centre . . .

Roberts, once a prolific goalscorer, but now approaching the end of
his career, had not finished the season, having been involved in a
car-crash and with no experienced centre-forward and with James
succumbing to injury, Preston's promotion bid foundered in the last
weeks of the season. However, by December of the following season they were in second place behind Chelsea, with Manchester
City in third place and James again leading the way. The *Lancashire
Daily Post* reported in February 1928:

> James was, of course, the prime mover in the advances and the
> variety of his ruses was only equalled by the accuracy of his
> placing. His opponents never knew whether he was going to hold
> or manoeuvre with the ball or turn it in the required direction by
> a free flick of the foot as it came to him and his capacity for being
> in the right position furnished a rare study in shrewd observation.

But Second Division football was hard, sometimes brutal, and the
physical demands were beginning to take their toll on Preston's
lightly-built Scots, and on James in particular:

> James's ankles come in for such attention from opponents that
> the Scot likes to give them salt-water treatment when he can. On
> a wintry day at Blackpool at Christmas when it was freezing hard,
> James did what few people would have ventured – walked for a
> mile along the shore in ice-cold water.

In January 1928 Hughie Gallacher was just beginning a two-month
suspension for retaliating against aggressive play. Hughie would
never learn to suffer in silence as his old friend did, but it was clear
that a great deal of the fun was going out of James's game. In
October, in an article contributed to the *Lancashire Daily Post*, he
took a wider look at the Second Division and the 'grim struggle' to
gain promotion. While there were some sides that tried to play good
football,

> I have also bumped up against sides playing the typical Second
> Division stuff of a few years back – football without frills on it.

And goodness knows these Second Division teams which cut out frills take a bit of beating. They play at 'the pace which kills' and woe betide the player with a scientific turn of mind who wants time in which to think out his moves. He doesn't get it!

Early in December of that year it was reported that James was tired of the Second Division: he answered reporters by saying that he was quite happy, 'even if he did get battered about more than any man cares for at times, owing to the type of game he effects'. He was now a definite target for 'hard men' and the Second Division had plenty of those.

Preston's two defeats by Barnsley were typical of this approach. Barnsley were described as having 'rude virtues'. They simply rolled their sleeves up and waded in: 'The old spirit of defiance shaped much of what they did; the grit was there, the determination to crush the other fellows' play out of shape and bend the game to their own whim.' One can almost feel the bone-shuddering shoulder-charges reverberating down the years.

'Perseus', summing up yet another unsuccessful season, laid the failure this time on Preston's lack of 'grit':

'On occasions the Preston side played almost as finely as any eleven could hope to do today. It was felt that no team capable of rising to such heights had any right to be remaining in the lower division.' However, they were 'too apt to be upset by opponents who stood on no ceremony. And above all, they were sadly lacking in tenacity.'

During the season 'Perseus' reckoned, '34 times was a lead reduced or lost and in six cases it resulted in the sacrifice of points: three losses and three draws. A three-goal lead against Manchester City and a five-four win achieved after Wolves had reduced the lead four times.'

Thus, though one hundred goals were scored, which was equalled only by Manchester City, champions of the Second Division and Everton, champions of the First, Preston remained in fourth place. They had missed promotion the previous season because of a weak attack; now the blame was laid on the defence.

Hopes that the 1928/29 season would combine the virtues of both were to be in vain. Russell was injured as early as September and would miss most of the season; Roberts had been transferred. Preston once again played well until December and were in the leading group, but from New Year's Eve onwards they would win only 13 more points and finish a disappointing 13th – an unlucky number in more ways than one. Long before the end of the season, controversy and rancour had engulfed the club; in March, almost the whole team was placed on the transfer list and *Athletic News* ran the headlines:

'HAS THE SCOTSMAN FAILED?'
Preston's Costly Experiment
A Warning

The club programme, however, carried the following explanation:

> The directors feel that some of the players have not fitted in with the scheme of things and have not, in fact, tried to arrive at the happy situation that tends to win matches by co-ordinated methods. Some of the team have been suffering from 'nerves' as a result and in consequence the best has not been seen of any of them . . .
> We must have a patriotic and loyal North End, a North End that is anxiously concerned about promotion as the directors and spectators are . . .

By blaming the players, the directors, Taylor in particular, appeared to have absolved themselves of all responsibility; supporters of the club, especially the shareholders, were not prepared to accept such an explanation and much of the criticism was inevitably aimed at Taylor:

> Either the board as a whole is in ignorance or is oblivious to the duties and necessities of its position or allowed itself to be dominated by one or two of its members who have the force to impose their ideas upon it.
> 'Preston Supporter Speaks Out' in *Thomson's Weekly News*,
> March 1929

Lack of team-building, general mismanagement, too great a reliance on Scotsmen – the criticisms would continue for years and Taylor would weather them all.

The decision to sell Alex James made a month earlier, before the general clear-out was announced, was the last straw for many, although his departure appeared to be due to matters entirely different from those in the director's statement.

Athletic News commented:

> It would be a mistake to infer that the Scotsman is not suited to English football or that he has failed. Preston seem to have over-indulged, having regard to the strenuous nature of Second Division play.
>
> Far more caution is needed in the transplantation of players and building of teams. Times have changed. English football is now more trying for the imported player. All the same it needs his style and skill.

9

Proud Preston

Dame rumour has been busy of late with the name of Alec James, Preston North End's clever inside forward. It is said that he wants to leave Preston and return to his native heath; I met Alec the other day and asked him if he was feeling the call of the heather and the hills.

'I don't know where the stories come from', he said. 'I don't want to leave England. I am one of the few Scotsmen who don't want to go home just yet. I am perfectly happy in England.' *Thomson's Weekly News*, 27 March 1931

PROFESSIONAL FOOTBALLERS OF the interwar period have often been portrayed as deferential, forelock-tugging servants, queueing up like schoolchildren to receive £5 bonuses from beaming directors. Yet it must be said that life for many players was unashamed bliss.

Although the crueller destitution of the early 1920s – ex-soldiers hawking their medals on street corners or selling home-made soap from door to door – had passed by the end of the decade, mass unemployment continued to impoverish substantial sections of the population of towns like Preston, dependent on stable industries like cotton and coal.

When Preston closed each year for Wakes Week and trains of excursionists travelled to Blackpool and the Lake District, many thousands more were left behind, too poor to join in the fun. Their lives were one long wake.

Yet even for those in work, summer-time brought none of the indulgent relaxation open to footballers. They were truly a privileged caste, leading lives that would only become the norm for working people in the 1950s.

Thomson's Weekly News encouraged footballers to write letters for publication during the close season, telling readers what they were up to. To the weary factory-hand or miner or out-of-work mill operative it must have seemed like paradise (albeit of a distinctly male kind).

Golf was, inevitably, the favourite hobby for most men, plus long lazy days at the race-course; others were pottering about in their gardens or away camping; cricket was a popular pastime – some players being good enough to represent their counties and thus earn themselves another substantial wage; some occupied themselves with fishing, twiddling with crystal radio sets, decorating the back room or moving into a new house. Motoring was now popular – one player recounted his first experience with a burst tyre. Foreign tours were commonplace: in 1927 Blackburn and Burnley were leisurely trouncing Dutch and German sides.

The summer of 1927 saw the James family taking themselves off to Scotland: Alex, his wife Peggy, son Alec plus his parents-in-law. But not to Mossend. He very soon established a pattern to his trips across the border, combining the best of both his worlds.

By 1927 his mother was dead; his father would die in 1928. The family home of Caledonian Buildings would then be vacated and, apart from occasional visits to his brothers and sisters, there would be no reason for him to stay long in his old home town.

Instead, he would head for Kirkcaldy and the golf courses of Fife. Bob Morrison provided a warm welcome and a comfortable house and, thus ensconced, James could divide his time between the links (where he watched the Open Golf Championships; closely studying the play of Bobby Jones, before taking up the clubs himself) and his old haunts and friends in Glasgow. Summer was the occasion for a gathering of the exiled football clans at various finals and celebrations; in 1927 James informed the *Weekly News* readers that he had watched his old junior club, Ashfield, play his old home town, Bellshill, before hurrying off to watch the Junior Cup Final at Hamden: he often did a little amateur talent-spotting. In fact, Preston signed on a local Kirkcaldy boy named Swallow on his recommendation.

But the golf was the main thing; by 1928, he had improved to the point where he won the consolation prize at the Footballer's Golf Tourney at Troon.

And if Scotland was for summer holidays and old friends, Preston was now for work and home in a neat little terraced house in Holmslack, close to the Deepdale ground.

Preston, along with many other northern towns of the interwar period, had suffered from being thought of as a place of gloom, depression and hopelessness. Life, we are led to believe, consisted of the dole, poverty and football – yet such an exaggerated picture does the town a great disservice.

That Preston was proud of its football team is undisputed; but football was just one aspect of life. Prestonians had much else to be proud of in a civic sense and were able to display that pride, and demonstrate that distinctive sense of identity through its unique Merchants' Guild, granted by charter in 1179. Indeed, it has been said that Prestonians tend to measure time by the famous Guild celebrations that occur every 20 years or so and, if a certain year is mentioned to a fellow Prestonian, he or she will remember marching in the Guild procession, getting married or its marking some other event in their lives.

Thus, 1922 might well have been recalled by the men and women in Fishergate not as the last occasion on which Preston reached the Cup Final but as the year of the last Guild; a time of fireworks and open-air dancing, of torch-lit processions and an historical pageant performed by eleven thousand school-children; of manufacturers and trades unions, merchants and apprentices, inheritors of the old trades companies, parading in aprons emblazoned to their crafts, examples of their skill borne on strikingly coloured and decorated vehicles; of men wearing flowing, broad-coloured sashes, medals and insignia of Buffalo Lodges or religious denominations, butchers in blue smocks leading beribboned sheep-dogs, printers and other tradesmen on flat-topped carts pulled by horses, men dressed as dancing bears . . .

All the world is at Preston – the multitude spreads,
So that through each street, 'tis a pavement of heads.

A distinctive town, therefore, with a distinctive character. For the James family of father, mother, son and soon baby daughter, it was a place to consolidate, to establish a family routine: a routine that left Peggy James very much on her own.

Being the wife of a footballer meant, if not exactly a life of ease (with two children to bring up life is never that easy), at least one without the need to venture out and find work. Thus, it was a genteel, lower-middle-class existence which offered her little chance of mixing with local people or with local professional society. She

CHELSEA PLAYERS UNDER THE MICROSCOPE

TOPICAL TIMES

NO. 477. [REGISTERED AS A NEWSPAPER AT G.P.O.]   WEEK ENDING JANUARY 5, 1929.   PRICE 2D.

Alec James At Home

Alec James, Preston North End's talented inside-left, as he appears off the football field. Here he is seen with his baby girl.

took little part in the life of the town or in the life of Preston North
End.

Her life centred around the two children – Alec Junior and Patsy,
born in 1928. Her father had been nonplussed by the arrival of a
girl:

> He was a little put out, I gather. What do you do with a girl? That
> was his attitude. And that's how I got my name, Patsy. After the
> Celtic footballer. It was a compromise – as I wasn't a boy, then
> I had to be named after a footballer!

He was a bit annoyed to find out later that my mother had entered the name as Patricia.

Peggy recalls that she never saw a game of football while at Preston,
and when the team was away her only company consisted of other
young footballers' wives who would come round to stay, bringing
their children with them:

> Lots of girls didn't like the life at all; if you had young children
> it could be terribly lonely, what with the special training
> weekends and never seeing him at Christmas and New Year. It
> was all right for the players, of course, put up in nice hotels close
> to golf-courses. But for the women it was the radio, if you had
> one, and the children.
>
> Alec always said to me, 'I'd never have been a great footballer
> if I hadn't married you'. By which I suppose he meant that, being
> the daughter of a football trainer, I understood all the comings
> and goings. I'd seen it all before, in fact, we'd lived something
> of a gypsy existence when I was a girl, travelling up and down
> the country. We must have moved house half a dozen times, at
> least, so I was used to the disruption. My father was never
> satisfied: when he was in football he said he hated it and wanted
> to get out, and vice versa.
>
> Alec was a great lover of his home when he was in it. But he
> wasn't really a 'home' person, not in the sense of fixing things
> or pottering about in the garden. If a tap dripped, he would send
> for a plumber. He loved the children, he would take them any-
> where. He would take little Alec to the Preston ground and take
> him into the dressing-room where he would have a nip of brandy
> or whisky, whatever it was they had at half-time to pep them up!

He had his own little seat on which to watch the match. Alec was proud of the children and very particular about their clothes – not that he would ever do anything about them, mind! But he was the sort of father who would stand little Alec on the table to straighten his socks, that sort of thing. And clean shoes! He was fussy about that. His sisters back in Bellshill used to clean his shoes for him, so he told me, but that was one thing I never did. But he would be in and out, restless all the time, and you never knew when to expect him.

While outside the factory hooters and bells sounded to summon the multitude to work, the James family had no need to hurry over breakfast. Peggy James's routine would be tailored to the children and each day was regulated by the arrival of tradesmen and delivery-boys:

> When milk was delivered in Preston it would be poured into jugs left on the doorstep. The jugs were covered with a saucer or little lace doilies. I remember some people had them with beads round the edges to hold them down to protect the milk from birds and cats.
>
> There were so many traditional street cries, you could set your clock by some of them! The rag-and-bone man, the coal-man, the chimney sweep and the ice-cream man. The ice-cream man came with a big churn on a horse-drawn cart and made you wafers as requested – later on there were men on sorts of tricycles who wore white coats and peaked caps. During the General Strike I remember how eery it was; the town seemed to go dead. Instead of coal, some-one came round selling squares of peat on carts.
>
> And people still wore clogs! Some of them were beautifully made, with steel tips that made sparks when they scuffed them!

But it was also a time of change, when even ordinary house-wives were becoming more assertive, some taking the controversial step of having their hair bobbed. Peggy had her hair cut short, but her husband was unimpressed:

> He just wanted me to be neat and tidy, really. He didn't like make-up, or painted finger-nails – not on me, anyway. He would say, as long as you wash your face and comb your hair, you're all

right. He was very traditionally Scottish in that way, in his
attitude towards his wife. But whatever I wanted to wear, if the
money was there, I could have it. Alec was never mean.

And it was in Preston that Alex James' own sartorial tastes began
to blossom. The 'flashy little Scot', as an acquaintance of his at the
time described him, would always take great care over his suits and
jackets; and it was in Preston that he was to alter his hairstyle from
the close-cropped Twenties cut that stood up like an urchin's and
helped to perpetuate his 'kid' image, to the more fashionable centre-
parting, smoothed-down look so favoured by stars of the silver
screen.
It was in Preston that he bought his first car.

It wasn't a gift, like some cars were, from directors to players as
a sort of under-the-counter payment. Ours came out of wages.
James Taylor, the club chairman, had two daughters and they
could drive, and one of them taught Alec. I remember going out
with them all: I went with Mr Taylor and we followed Alec who
was with one of the daughters who was showing him how to drive
the thing. We went to Blackpool or Southport I think . . .

Car-ownership among professional footballers was a measure of
how far ahead their disposable income was of the working-class
population's. In April, 1928, it was reported that at least five of the
Manchester United team had motor cars and along with the cars
(not to mention the motor cycles) came accidents.
    The most prestigious soccer victim to date had been Dixie Dean.
In June 1926 his motor cycle (with girl-friend behind as pillion passenger) collided head-on with an oncoming motor bike and side-
car in North Wales, breaking Dean's jawbone in two places; for a
time it was thought he had fractured his skull. He was unconscious
for 36 hours and was lucky to survive. (And thus was born the
legend of his phenomenal heading powers being due to a metal plate
inserted in his skull!)
    Closer to home, of course, had been the accident that helped ruin
Preston North End's promotion run in 1927 when Alex Jackson's
car went off the road on fog-shrouded Pennine moorland and injured three of Preston's most costly acquisitions.
    Jackson recalled the sight when he came to:

Struggling to my feet I looked around and was appalled at the sight which met my eyes. A few feet away from me I could dimly discern the form of Willie Russell stretched out as if he were dead. My brother Walter and Tom Roberts also seemed unnaturally quiet.

Alex James could have been in that car; in fact, it was his erratic time-keeping that had caused the men to miss their train and thus chance their lives in Alex Jackson's dashing new sportscar.

Jackson and company were lucky to avoid damaging publicity; motor car accidents were big news in the 1920s and 30s; with cars being such a relatively rare form of public transport, those inside them were usually well-off or famous – in either case, newsworthy.

That increasing numbers of footballers were joining the ranks of private motorists also emphasised the extent to which they were becoming divorced from the lives of those around them. Before the First World War, being better paid simply meant a temporarily better standard of living; it didn't offer the means of escape from the milieu from which one had sprung. Closed railway carriages and exclusive hydros were temporary things; the percentage of professional footballers who continued in their original trades was quite high and thus the world of work and day-to-day events, of politics, still intruded. The year of 1909 had seen a strong, vocal Players Union attempt to take on the League and the FA in a struggle for, among other things, freedom of contract, joining hands with the Trades Union movement of the day – even going on strike.

But since that defeat, footballers had retreated and had allowed themselves to be shepherded into an increasingly unreal world running parallel with the 'real' one. The once-strong Players Union met in Manchester in August 1927 with just 11 delegates representing a mere 150 players. Jimmy Fay, the secretary, was waging a gallant fight against the tall odds of indifference.

Players still continued to give time and energy raising money for charities and distress funds: Preston North End played regular friendlies to raise money for the Preston Unemployed League, and James played alongside David Jack and Dixie Dean in aid of the Fleetwood Distress Fund in November 1927. But though not oblivious to the outside world, they were becoming less and less *of* it.

They were certainly the objects of veneration for a generation of schoolboys now being fed a diet of pulp magazines and newspapers such as *Sports Budget, Football Favourite and Topical Times*. Boys would scrabble about among the tides of litter left by football crowds searching for empty cigarette cartons containing precious picture cards on which would be printed highly-coloured, almost surreal portraits of the 'stars'.

Leslie Knopp was 12 when he first saw Alex James. He was taken to each home match by his father who, by dint of owning a few shares, could afford to buy a season ticket in the main stand. Together they would walk the short distance from their home in St Paul's Road to the Deepdale ground:

James had no great reputation when he first came. Willie Russell was a more prestigious buy, and my own hero, if you could call him that, had been Joe McCall who had been at Preston some years before and whom I must have seen when I was no more than six or so. A truly great player.

Yet when James left Preston, it was a great shock to the town. There had been plenty of rumours and people knew it had to happen eventually – my father teased me, in fact, on one occasion. There was a Leslie James who played the organ in the local cinema and he left rather suddenly and I well remember my father asking me one Saturday on the way to the ground, 'Have you heard? James has gone.' I was so upset, I nearly went back home until he laughed and said, 'I mean Leslie!'

Knopp never met his idol. Harry Parker, son of one of Preston's directors, was luckier:

You nearly curtsied when you met him! He was the King of Preston, because he was unique. He did things on the football field that no one else had ever done. The way he waggled his foot over the ball leaving the ball untouched but sending the opponent toppling! People loved to watch things like that. They came in their thousands to see him: it was like a modern dance step! That little hesitation and side-step before setting off on a dribble – like the Charleston!

I remember once he scored a goal – he'd got through to the goalkeeper and instead of crashing it, he feinted to shoot hard on one side, then calmly side-footed it the other! And the crowd didn't know whether to laugh or to cheer!

Harry Parker's father was a master baker; the Parker shop was close to the ground:

> In St Paul's Road, surrounded by mills, we'd sell 350 meat and potato pies every lunchtime. I was lucky – I had all I wanted: money, my own car. An MG! And I used to drive Alec about before he got his own car. My father would say, 'Drive Alec here or there.' I just acted like a chauffeur. There wasn't much in Preston by way of clubs, you see: you had to go to Manchester or Blackpool for those . . .
>
> Alec struck me then as a brash little chap; he dressed loudly – tweeds, bow-tie, baggy trousers, a little Scots beret or cap on his head. He would help out with the coaching of the third team, sometimes: I never graduated beyond that into the reserves and I can remember him now, calling out to me, 'Come on, Harry, you're not putting currants into buns now, you know!'
>
> He was always up to something. Dad said to me one day 'I want you to meet Alec at the ground and do what he tells you.' He had a Standard Eight then, lovely little car. I followed him out of Preston and we drove up on to Bligsdale Fell. When we were on our own, Alec took out a can of petrol and poured it over the engine and then put a match to it! I never did find out why, insurance perhaps, behind on the payments. Anyway, a farmer came along on a bloody tractor and thought we needed help and put the bugger out! So we had to drive all the way back again.
>
> He was a funny little man, but he could be a bit abrasive at times. I was playing billiards with a friend in the recreation room at the club one day when Alec came in with a new player – Chalmers, I think it was. He didn't wait for us to finish, he just scattered the balls on the table and said, 'Bugger off!'. And we did.

That he was a joker off the pitch as well as on is undisputed. Newspapers regularly carried tales of his pranks, acted out on lonely railway stations to amuse the rest of the team as they waited for interminable connections:

'Alec James, the prime humourist of the Preston North End team, was "snapped" on the Sheffield station recently while wearing a station newsboy's cap and carrying the lad's newspapers and magazines – ' and very rarely was he upstaged, though one station porter at Todmorden managed it:

> Anyone who can match Alec James for spontaneous wit is a 'guid
> yin' but the porter is at least Alec's equal. When James stood on
> the platform seat and pretended to be a bookmaker calling out
> the odds, the railwayman made a mock grimace and said, 'Come
> off there – I get £2 a week for being the fool here.'

Acting the fool for a bet was a James speciality, and it is a measure
of how times have changed that his colleagues were prepared to
wager money on his not having the courage to walk the streets of
the sleepy town of Matlock dressed in plus fours, spats and wearing
Dave Morris's bowler hat – on a Sunday. Needless to say, he won
the bet.

But Alex James liked to enjoy himself. If he was not driving his
new car or playing pranks on his team-mates, he might be making
the rounds of the cinemas in Preston, a routine that would often include Peggy and the children. At home, the gramophone now had
a collection of dance tunes, while in the corner of the sitting-room
the latest radio set crackled to the sounds of London life: the Savoy
Dance Band, Ambrose and his Orchestra, Jack Payne, Henry Hall
– and, occasionally, the voice of Herbert Chapman, the innovatory
Arsenal manager, delivering one of his regular talks on football, and
its exciting future.

10

Wee Blue Devils

England were not merely beaten. They were bewildered – run to a standstill; made to appear utterly inferior footballers by a team whose play was as cultured and beautiful as I ever expect to see.
Ivan Sharpe, 'Wee Blue Devils' in *Athletic News*, April 1928

BY 1928 JAMES was 26 years old, a player in his prime physically; he had spent some six years in top-grade football and had an international cap. But Hughie Gallacher had achieved so much more and so much faster. With Airdrie he had won a Scottish Cup medal; with Newcastle he had won a League Championship medal. He had also represented Scotland on ten occasions, not to mention winning Scottish League caps. James was never one to covet awards and medals: he had no cabinet at home to display them; nor was he a jealous man. But he was increasingly concerned that he should advance in the game in order to make progress towards achieving some sort of financial security.

For what was rapidly becoming clear was his penchant for the very best things in life: situations, acquaintances – even acquisitions.

Because he was a sought-after player, admired and valuable, the barriers that might normally have existed between directors and players were regularly breached by James. He was often to be seen in the company of men far richer than himself, men who, though usually associated with football in some way, had built up prosperous businesses for themselves. James was thus one of their 'perks': they courted him, were flattered to be seen in his presence.

For his part, James rarely stood on ceremony for he saw himself as the equal of any man, no matter how rich, and he usually managed to speak his mind. To that extent he was ambitious, and not particularly content with his lot.

But it was only on the football field that he really controlled matters; there his confidence and sure-footedness led to almost absolute domination of those around him. Off the field, he was at the mercy of others.

What was doubly frustrating for James and for many top footballers was that the 1920s and 1930s saw certain sportsmen and women rapidly becoming as well paid as film-stars and music-hall celebrities. As part of the growing entertainment industry, sports were beginning to 'take off', especially in America.

Although the money paid in transfers for footballers was entering the five-figure era, still very little of it trickled down to the men concerned; this had long been a bone of contention particularly when it was clear that their presence in the side sometimes added many hundreds of pounds a week onto the week's takings. (Where James was concerned, it was estimated that he added £300 a week to Preston's receipts.)

Such players could look up at the stands being built and watch the directors enjoying drinks and hospitality in the board room (Masonic handshakes all round) and feel not a little aggrieved.

With the new popular sports press feeding off gossip and sensation, they could also see that boxers, golfers, baseball stars and tennis stars were earning what were, by anyone's standards, small fortunes.

In 1927, tennis stars such as Suzanne Lenglen and Bill Tilden were in the news: Lenglen had turned professional and was receiving vast sums from C. B. Cochrane to perform exhibition matches (at Blackpool, for instance, before audiences of seven thousands) while Tilden was being offered £20,000 to do likewise. The stars of James's second sporting love – golf – were also earning extremely good salaries while jockeys such as Steve Donaghue and George Bullen were rich enough to afford small aeroplanes. Boxers (including local Bellshill boy Tommy Milligan, in 1927 the conqueror of Ted Moore and returning home in triumph) were battling it out for large purses, while baseball stars such as Babe Ruth were said to be on the dollar equivalent of £15,000 a year. Even cricketers received between £10 and £15 a match, while football managers such as Chapman and Peter McWilliam at Spurs could expect anything between £1,500 and £2,000 a year.

Professional footballers, however, were prevented from earning more than £8 basic a week. Thus, the comment in the *Topical Times* of 1926: 'The professional footballer appears poor by comparison with the participants of other sports, yet his lines are often cast in pleasant places,' must have raised a rueful smile.

Somehow, professional footballers continued to pay a price for having been the first to breach the social taboos all those years ago in the 1880s – for having divorced sport from the purely educational, character-building role the reformers and educators had marked out for it. Professional footballers were credited with having turned a game into a commercial thing – an unfair stigma. There was certainly a price paid in social terms: golfers, tennis-players, jockeys, even boxers appeared more acceptable to the middle and upper classes and royalty itself, than footballers. Rugby Union had even been dubbed more 'patriotic' and was encouraged in public schools – as if the very soccer code was somehow tainted and vulgar.

Sadly, the millions who flocked to watch the game were often ambivalent towards their heroes' aspirations. Perhaps the game was too close to the people from which it had sprung, so that jealousy and resentment prevented the average working man from supporting the players in their struggle for freedom of contract. Certainly in 1909, when the Players Union had stood firm, very few of the public seemed keen to support them. 'What more do they want?' appeared to have been the sentiment. 'Lucky buggers . . .'

The world of football finance remained a murky twilight one, with the FA and the League appearing to have total control of it and certainly possessing draconian powers to punish those caught transgressing the arcane rules and regulations restricting players' pay.

But with cash flowing in abundance through the turnstiles and into the bank accounts of rich, amateur directors who were more than happy to finance their pet hobby, such control was at best haphazard, sometimes no more than a veneer on a very bumpy surface. Certainly the mass of average players, with no union to organise them and articulate their grievances, and with precious little individual bargaining power (one look over their shoulders at the legion of unemployed just begging for a chance to pull on their boots could tell them that) were firmly under control. But star players were commodities who possessed market value and, in a society otherwise free of controls, that value could usually be realised in cash.

Alex James, in mid-career at Preston, though professing to be happy with his lot and content to be a big fish in a little pool, was aware that his personal stock was for ever rising: 'All the rumours flying around were very unsettling. I don't pretend to know all that was going on behind the scenes, but I believe the offers made very, very tempting.'

Doubts about his physical ability to withstand the strain of English football had now all but disappeared; but, more significantly, his reappearance on the international scene in March 1928 was to more than confirm his status as a desirable commodity – as well as put his name on the lips of millions.

Since his unfortunate debut in 1925 against Wales, James had remained on the international sidelines. With two great Scottish inside forwards in Andy Cunningham and Tommy Cairns of Rangers there was no need for the selectors to look very far for inside lefts, and between 1920 and 1926 Scotland dominated the England–Scotland series, winning four and drawing two.

But in 1927, with Cunningham approaching the end of his international career and Cairns already gone, Scotland lost to England at Hampden of all places, beaten by a combination of Dixie Dean (on his debut in the big game and scoring two goals) and a stubborn defence. Though Scotland played well, this defeat by the English side rankled, particularly as England had played the second half with Hill, captain and centre-half, as a virtual passenger. 'Broadcaster' wrote in the *Daily Express*: 'There were a number of English visitors wearing white rosettes in Argyle Street, as bold as brass and entirely unmolested. This is a joke.'

As the 1927/28 season progressed with James doing so well at Preston it seemed certain that the selection would come. The first international had been a 2-2 draw against Wales at Wrexham and the inside left for Scotland had been Stevenson, making his debut in international football. It had not been a bad result, as Wales was a strong side and would win the international championship that season.

However, in February 1928 James was selected for the match against Ireland to be held at Firhill Park, Glasgow. It was a crucial time for Preston in the League – challenging for promotion and looking likely to achieve it – so James was 'asked' whether he wanted to play against Ireland.

No one expected him to choose country before club, as the inter-

national clashed with a vital promotion match with Manchester
City, who were certainly not going to allow their Scottish player,
Jimmy McMullen, to be released. Thus, as the *Lancashire Daily
Post* put it, '(James) has placed himself, like the loyal servant and
good sportsman that he is, unreservedly in the hands of the directors and manager who will assume responsibility for the decision.'

They decided that James would miss the international. James
made no protest – he was in any case preoccupied with the death
of his father on that very weekend – and a small rueful-looking
cartoon of him appeared in the *Lancashire Daily Post*. Preston drew
the crucial match 2-2. Scotland lost to Ireland 1-0.

By March, however, the situation was entirely different. Scotland
was in something of a crisis. Without a win that season, and having
just seen the Scottish League team thrashed 6-2 by the English

League, it was a time of anguish and wailing. The English, it was claimed, were faster, fitter, more decisive . . .

The fact cannot be hidden that we were beaten for speed and, be it said, finesse . . . The English were as scientific as our fellows and really blew the tradition of superior cleverness sky high. In fact, it caused one to wonder whether we have not made far too much of this and caused our players to develop into a lot of slow-coaches . . .

The English, 'Meander' continued, did in one move what the Scots took four to accomplish.

This may sound like heresy but for the life of me I cannot see why the Scottish style cannot be maintained at a greater velocity than nowadays we are accustomed to. Therefore, let us have a team of live merchants with snap and pace about them.

Unfortunately, this led to an ominous conclusion: the trials had demonstrated that 'the Anglos had greater nippiness about them than our home men and were, therefore, likelier to counter the English method'. Further, it demonstrated that certain of them were full of ability . . . none more so than James.

Alec James was the star turn. He was playing in the district which idolised him as an Ashfield junior and whence as a mere boy he left to have his senior baptism with the Raith Rovers. In those days and up till the time he left Starks Park for Deepdale he was 'too fond of the ball'. His contact with English football has apparently knocked all the 'selfishness' out of him and his value has increased threefold. He has undoubtedly the 'punch' so sadly lacking in the Scottish international attacks this season.

Glasgow Evening Times, 14 March 1928

Thus, there was no escaping the awkward fact – the Scots team would have to contain a majority of Anglos: 'It goes against the grain to find oneself preferring so many Anglo-Scots, but necessity is a hard mistress.' The England-Scotland match was the ultimate conflict; and to fight a war, how much better to fight it with patriots rather than mercenaries. But in 1928 there was no escaping the fact

The Cup Final, 1930; Arsenal v Huddersfield Town, James is in the background on the left
watching as Cliff Bastin takes charge of the ball. (Illustrated London News)

Arsenal's first goal; from a free-kick James passed to Bastin on the left wing and the
latter first drew the defence, then passed inwards again to James who scored with a low
hard drive that gave the goalkeeper no chance. (Illustrated London News)

James knew that he had to cash in on his image, which he did with varying degrees of success. He was a sports demonstrator for Selfridges (above), opened a sweet and tobacco shop near the Arsenal ground in 1935 and turned out for Friern Barnet Grammar, his son's school team, in 1939, Alex junior was in goal. (Selfridges, Associated Press, Illustrated London News)

that the massive spending spree of the preceding three years by
English clubs had removed the cream of Scottish talent south. When
the team for the international was announced, there were only three
'home' Scots selected – a famous cartoon depicts the three leaving
Glasgow Station, bemoaning the fact that they were one short for a
cards foursome. Underlying everything, of course, was the disturbing thought that
English methods were now in the ascendant; victory, even if it could
be achieved, would be bought at a price. 'Anglos', playing the
English game . . .

For this match of matches, the Preston board offered no resistance to James – indeed, the manager and four directors accompanied him down on the day. Preston North End, the *Weekly News*
declared, was taking no chances with its star player.

The Scots, meanwhile, were gathering in London, the biennial
invasion now having become a ritual, much puzzled over by
Englishmen and some Scots:

> Now it is rather startling to find such douce buddies as Kirk elders
> and banktellers flaunting garish tartan tammies and flying
> Scottish favours in the Strand on a Saturday morning and
> possibly going gite in the afternoon if Gallacher scores a goal at
> Wembley. In the minds of the public there seems to be some
> association between putting a tammy over one's head and straw
> in it.

Bagpipes skirled over London from dawn onwards; James even
claimed that a piper had stood outside the team hotel and played all
night: 'Nothing could stop him. We had to lie awake and put up with
it.'

Next morning, as trainload after trainload of bedraggled and be-
fuddled Scots filtered out into London and, it seemed, into the
team's hotel, which swarmed with well-wishers and hangers-on,
Alex James and Alex Jackson took themselves off to the England
team hotel to 'needle' their opponents. Four of the England team
were Huddersfield Town men, team-mates of Jackson's: 'We
started kidding them on as to what would happen to them that afternoon . . . we bragged for all we were worth. They were going to see
football as it should be played . . . I wonder they put up with us.'

And while this rather novel form of pre-match preparation was taking place, the clans were gathering along the Wembley Way.

It was a wet blustery day, 'sometimes blazing sun and a hot atmosphere, and anon icy blasts and lowering clouds,' but as a thousand 'paper glengarries' were fashioned, the stewards distributed song sheets and 'a man with a mission and a megaphone . . . coaxed and later goaded the crowd to show what they could do in the vocal line . . .'

All the time the rain fell heavily on to the thick, lush turf – a factor that would prove of great significance as the game progressed. And as the crowd warmed to the task:

> responding lustily to the lead given by the band and conduct-
> or, 'Tipperary', 'Who's your lady fair?', 'Loch Lomond' were
> heartily voiced! and hearing these in London brought memo-
> ries back to many who had passed through Victoria in the War
> days . . .

Down in the dressing-room, the mounting excitement, deafening roars and fervent atmosphere seemed not to have touched Alex James. He had a difficult decision to make; as *Thomson's Weekly News* reported:

> Although a Scot, Alec James would never be happy in a kilt
> for he hates to have his knees exposed. For the match at Wem-
> bley he was provided by the North End manager with a pair of
> satinette pants. When Alec came to don them, however, he
> found they were some inches shorter than the 'plus fours' he
> had always favoured. Looking at the new shorts with disdain,
> Alec declared that he wasn't going to wear them. 'I should look
> a kid in these,' he commented. And he didn't wear them.

And, at last, the teams emerged, led by captain McMullen, filmed by the Pathé News (a lone cameraman cranking away) out into the drizzle where the Duke of York shook their hands while Scots mascot bearers conducted a running battle with London bobbies.

England kicked off and the crowd, though drenched and cold, were immediately plunged into frantic action. Within two minutes, the English winger Smith broke through, cut inside and shot against the upright – the ball rebounded into play with no English forward there to put it into the net.

Two minutes later, James released Morton on the left, the 'Wee
Society Man' dashed to the byline and cut the ball back, head high.
Alex Jackson met it at the near post heading smartly home! A goal
in five minutes! Through the drenching rain, the first sounds of
singing could be heard.

But for the next half hour there was to be no glorious Scottish
exhibition; instead, an enthralling battle, a clash of styles, the out-
come of which was in doubt as long as Dean was thundering through
to meet crosses supplied by Joe Hulme and Smith, while Gallacher
was tempting centre-half Wilson out of position and luring him into
rash tackles . . .

For a long while the Scots were pressed back in their own half,
James and Dunn, the Scottish inside forwards, battling to support
their half-back lines, and had England equalised during the thrills
and spills of this period of pressure, no one could have complained.
But, somehow, Dean failed to find the net – the ball either headed
over the bar or into the arms of Harkness, the Scots keeper, who
risked life and limb diving at the feet of the oncoming English forwards more than once.

And as the turf became more slippery and slidey, it was clear that
the little Scots forwards were playing a game that suited: short trian-
gular movements up each wing, always two or three men in support. Increasingly, the English defenders, accustomed to the ground
underneath turning to mud in such weather, mud being a surface
upon which they could safely launch themselves, found instead
their footing was uncertain, turning being fraught with danger: and
the Scots forwards were for ever releasing the ball in quick efficient
movements that rendered the English tackles clumsy, ill-timed,
Gallacher and Dunn and Morton all being brought down from
behind in penalty-appealing circumstances.

And, with five minutes of the first half left, there came the
decisive strike:

Manoeuvring for position at 30 yards out, James veered to the
right. Wilson seemed to impede his path. He might have stopped
an ordinary individual but James is not that sort of chap. He had
learned a particularly fine side-step back in his Saracen Park days
and brought it into service. The bait was successful, Wilson did
not know where he had gone, Hufton did not know how he was
coming. Both were lost. The shot went like a rocket away past

the keeper's right and the Tam o' Shanters brigade went delirious with joy.

Thus, at half-time, England was 2-0 down: the band played 'Keep The Home Fires Burning' and the Scots supporters, steaming and damp, were now in full sway: 'How the Scotties sang! Never in their lives had many had such occasion for letting rip. Never a thought of whether luck would hold, just hope for the best.'

But it was the English who were hoping for the best. The Scots supporters and players alike seemed gripped by a certainty – victory was secure. But more than that: a triumph!

The second half opened with a predictable English charge which failed. And, from then on, it was the exhibition the Scots had always dreamed of. Ivan Sharpe, greatest of interwar sports writers, editor of *Athletic News,* watched in awe:

> Real football at last! Clockwork passing. The 'triangle' – prettiest of all tunes football can provide – tinkling for an hour or so on both sides of the field; Gibson (at his best) behind Jackson and the little Dunn; McMullen (generally great in attack)

THE EVENING TIMES, SATURDAY, MARCH 31, 1928

ENGLAND "SCOTCHED"

GLORIOUS VICTORY
Scots Complete Masters at Wembley
JACKSON SCORES THREE AND JAMES TWO
The Old Alan Morton
HALF-BACKS BRILLIANT
ALL THE SCOTS DO WELL
(By THE "TIMES" EXPERTS)
SCOTLAND 5   ENGLAND 1

inspiring Morton and James. James! He needs no inspiration. But he got it and, taking the game through, was the mastermind of this clockwork Scottish forward line. Clockwork is the word. Take the fifth and last Scottish goal. Admittedly, it came at a time when England were down and out, but it shows how perfectly Scotland played. McMullen (left half back) had the ball 40 yards from the goal-line. I was over 100 yards away yet I heard the call of Morton (outside left) for the ball: 'Jimmy-y'. No sooner said than done. Between half back and back went the arrow-like ground pass. Morton racing ahead in anticipation caught it, eased up, crossed the ball a yard from the line and as it fell in front of goal Jackson running in met it in the air three yards from the post. Crash! A volley goal at point blank range. That is football – the real thing!

By the time the last Scottish goal was scored, community singing of the truly spontaneous kind had been rolling around the stadium for some half an hour.

To say the whole crowd was delighted with the Scots cleverness was beyond question as Cockney voices resounded with 'Go it, Scotland, you Devils!'

The ovation to the Scottish victors at the close was something to remember but, actually, for the last half an hour the crowds in the stands, particularly mostly English enthusiasts, were alternately shouting their approbation of the Scots, voicing admiration of their wizardry or laughing uproariously at their tricks.

Thus, to the sound of bagpipes, the Wee Blue Devils (Ivan Sharpe's article headline adopted for posterity) entered popular mythology.

At the end, the score stood at 5-1 and the team was engulfed in Scottish fans while the band, in bizarre fashion, yet somehow matching the mood of the bemused English players, played the Afghan national anthem.

Headlines in Scotland were ecstatic: 'England Scotched', 'Scotland Stands Where She Did', 'Soccer Object Lesson for England at Wembley'. And no one in England seemed to disagree.

Something in the enthusiasm of all those present, something about their joy, their drunken celebrations, suggests the release of pent-up frustration on behalf of so many soccer fans, tired of 'technique' and 'method', of 'utility' and 'planning'; and those joyous Scots supporters who flocked eagerly into London to be greeted as heroes and feted as though they were the ones who had scored the goals, were celebrating a victory of the spirit. It was catching:

London was a lovely place on Saturday night for Scots. There were 8,000 roistering but well-behaved Scots and everybody wanted to make a fuss over us.

London never saw such football before and couldn't tell us often enough. In the big restaurants and swagger-lounges in the evening, all the bands played Scottish music, every bit of tartan was uproariously greeted and every Scottish melody brought the orchestra salvoes of cheering.

We ought never to mention Bannockburn again after such a welcome . . . But it was easy enough to be pleasant when life – as represented by a wonderful game – went by like a song.

Glasgow Evening Times, 2 April 1928

11

Up for Sale

Until the season 1928/29 I never knew what trouble was at Preston. Then came the one and only cloud. And didn't the rumour-mongers make the most of it?   Alex James in *Thomson's Weekly News*, January 1931

IN APRIL 1928 Alex James presented the Preston North End board with a picture of himself shaking hands with the Duke of York before the England–Scotland match. A gift not without irony, for within six months he was having to apologise (on pain of suspension) to the same board for having publicly demonstrated his disdain for them. The 'one and only cloud' would continue to drizzle down on Preston for almost a season.

The trouble arose over the question of James's availability for selection for the Scottish team to play against Wales on 27 October 1928. The 'rumour-mongers' informed him that the board might not offer him the usual club or country choice: 'I had letters by every post from unknown fans in Scotland saying that I was going to be victimised by my club's anxiety to keep me for themselves.'

He confronted Gibson, Preston's manager, who told him not to worry: if he was picked for Scotland then he would be released. However, Scotland did not select him and although the directors claimed that they had not blocked his release, the Preston minutes state: '25th September, 1928, James refused permission to play in the Scotland v. Wales game on 27th Oct 1928.'

James had no access to the minutes, but it was clear that he had been deceived. He angrily refused to turn out for Preston again; the directors called his bluff and selected him for the next home match versus Swansea. The display he put on that day was a puzzle to all those unaware of the feud: the *Lancashire Daily Post* of 20 October reported: 'He allowed himself no flight of fancy, cut out all the ruses that are his stock in trade, turned the ball over much as it came to him; he was designedly a penny-plain footballer instead of a tuppenny or sixpenny coloured one . . .'

The crowd, bewildered at first to see their idol simply sidling about, indifferent to the action, soon vented their anger with boos and catcalls. James had delivered a calculated and embarrassing public snub to the board, who summoned him to an extraordinary meeting and asked him to explain himself.

James claimed that he had simply been unable to concentrate on the game, so worked up had he been over what he considered the 'injustice' done to him. The board demanded an apology; James apologised. The incident effectively ended his career at Preston North End.

Early in the New Year he was placed on the transfer list and, in February, it was announced to a shocked Preston public that Liverpool was on the brink of signing him. It was to be another six months, however, of ballyhoo, bluff and secret assignations before he was finally to leave Preston. As he put it: 'The only time a footballer can call his name and his ability his own is when it comes to that little matter of dipping a pen in the ink and writing a signature across the form.'

Clubs with illustrious pasts, the chance to earn championship medals, the opportunity to play with skilful players: none of these factors had the slightest influence on him – much to Preston's chagrin. He was concerned with just one thing: 'Dear old Jock Ewert, my playing pal, used to tell me: "Get all you can out of this racket. You're worth it. The people who come to watch Preston only come to see you. Cash in while you can".'

To coin the preferred football cliché: James was concerned to secure his future: 'Prominent players just then were being offered business opportunities in the larger towns. I was coming in for a good deal of favourable notice so why should my thoughts not turn to business, too?'

Exactly what sort of business he had in mind, he never made clear. He was possibly a little hazy about it himself.

At first, though, James made it as clear as he could (without actually saying so) that what he really wanted was a considerable amount of money, under the counter. Liverpool, first in the race, were either unable to read his rather crude sign language or simply unwilling to pay.

Next in line was Manchester City: early one morning, James was bundled into a car by manager Gibson and driven to Bolton where the Wanderers were playing Liverpool in the Cup:

'All the Manchester City board were at an hotel and we drove up in style. I walked into a room and there they were, sitting at a long table, waiting for the "slave" who was being bought and sold at an auction.'

But, once again, James could get no assurances that any extra cash was on offer. The problem now was, however, that Manchester City had offered Preston considerably more money than Liverpool – the reputed £15,000 – and the Preston people were understandably keen that James should sign. The club minutes state that the board 'were prepared to accept the City offer'; which made matters very awkward for James.

If a player simply continued to refuse transfer deals without good reason, the FA could assume he was asking for illegal money. The authorities were already watching the James transfer with some interest; suspension again loomed.

The Manchester City directors adjourned the negotiations in order to watch the cup tie match, but once the game was over they pressed James for an answer. Would he sign? No, he said, not before he had asked his wife.

'Right,' they said. 'You go and see your wife and meet us in the North End boardroom tonight,' assuming no doubt, that a wife would provide no obstacle. Then they drove away, leaving James stranded in Bolton with no means of getting back home except by train.

Fuming, James begged a lift from a football colleague and hurried back to Preston. Manchester City was obviously not going to offer him anything by way of financial inducements and only Peggy his wife could provide him with a sufficiently convincing excuse. Peggy decided to be awkward:

I told her that if anybody asked her she was to say she did not think Manchester would be good for the children's health and back that up by saying that she herself didn't want to go there.

'Who says I don't want to go to Manchester?' was her first question when I told her the carefully prepared alibi.

'I do!'

'You're crazy, Alec. Of course I'd like to go!'
'It doesn't matter whether you'd like to go or not. You say what
I tell you to say if anybody asks!'

Peggy claimed it was the only time she was ever 'consulted' about
affairs of business.

At the news that his wife was worried about the injurious
Manchester climate, the directors simply laughed. Easy, they said.
Live outside Manchester in a nice club house. James dodged about
desperately. Peggy, he claimed, had read in the papers that Jimmy
McMullen, City's captain, had had a lot of worry over his wife's
health and that of their children. She was adamant. The City
directors left.

The next morning James was summoned to Gibson's office to
answer the phone: 'Hullo, Alex, this is Jimmy McMullen! They tell
me you're coming to Manchester!' Like the loyal club captain he
was, McMullen tried hard to persuade James to change his mind
but to no avail. Fortunately, McMullen was a close friend and
promised to put Manchester City off the scent. But he had a final
word of warning: 'Watch your step when you do move. Certain folk
may try to make it awkward for you.'

As would often be the case, James had talked himself into an
awkward situation but he had no obvious means of extricating
himself. When he later turned down Aston Villa as well, it was clear
that whoever bought James would find the League management
committee keen to investigate the club books – hardly an induce-
ment for the majority of clubs in the First Division.

Thus it was strange, to say the least, that Arsenal FC should
emerge in the early spring as favourite to sign him.

While it is true that Herbert Chapman, Arsenal's manager, had
been searching for some time for a creative forward in the Clem
Stevenson tradition – indeed, had made enquiries almost a year
earlier concerning James – it was also the case that, in 1929, the
Arsenal Football Club was reeling from the trauma of losing one of
its founding directors, William Norris, – banned from involvement
in football *'sine die'* for alleged 'financial irregularities'. The
enquiry that had brought the abuses to light had taken place some
two years earlier but in 1929 Norris was suing the FA (unsuccess-
fully) for libel; details of the case had been leaked to the press and
Norris claimed his reputation had been impugned.

Central to the original case had been the allegation that illegal financial inducements had been paid to players to gain their signatures, and in particular a lump sum was said to have been paid to Charlie Buchan, Herbert Chapman's first signing upon taking over at Arsenal in 1925. Buchan had negotiated long and hard before agreeing to come to Arsenal, demanding compensation for giving up a shop he had in his native Sunderland. During the negotiations, Norris claimed, Chapman had pleaded with the chairman to pay what Buchan had wanted, but had left the room while the deed was actually done. Chapman subsequently denied all knowledge of the secret payments; Norris called him a liar. But then Chapman had good reason to distance himself from trouble.

Before he had become manager of Huddersfield in 1920, Chapman had been in charge of Leeds City from 1912 until 1918, on a part-time basis for the last two years, as he was also manager-in-chief of a wartime munitions factory. In December 1918 he had resigned from Leeds City to take up industrial management full time; in 1919, an enquiry into allegations that Leeds City had broken wartime regulations by paying players more than the permitted rates resulted in the club being expelled from the League. Chapman was barred, along with others, from attending football matches and taking any part in football management again.

Chapman's guilt was to remain a matter of conjecture – the Leeds club refused to reveal the books to the League, hence the decision to expel the club. Because Chapman had been absent for a considerable period of time due to his work at the munitions factory it has generally been assumed that he was the least involved of all the parties to the irregularities.

In 1920, then out of work, Chapman was approached by Huddersfield Town to go there as manager. He put his case to the League and it was decided to lift the suspension.

Chapman appears to have managed to sail extremely close to the wind throughout his career, without suffering disastrous consequences. Nonetheless, at the sight of Alex James heaving into view, decked out in gaudy bow-tie, George Raft spats and tartan titfer and with a negotiating style as discreet as his check-patterned plus fours, the League management committee must have wondered what they had done to deserve such good fortune. Arsenal and Chapman were obviously intent on committing football suicide.

But Alex James, renowned for his magical Houdini acts on the field of play, was about to perform just such an act (albeit with the help of some influential friends) off it.

James wrote in his memoirs, serialised in the *News of the World* in 1937, that he was unable to reveal the name of the man he regarded as responsible for arranging his transfer to Arsenal. The man, he claimed, was unwilling to come forward and take the plaudits – he was shy of publicity: 'The only way out, then, is for me to introduce to you "the mystery man behind Alec James" – Mr X'

Just why Mr X wished to remain anonymous is a puzzle, unless it was simply a desire on the part of the ghost-writers to beef up the James story for *News of the World* readers. Yet perhaps Mr X felt nothing would be gained by having his role in a highly contentious transfer deal examined in any detail; because Mr X was himself closely involved in the affairs of another League club – Bradford City.

Tom Paton – Mr X – was an extremely wealthy wool merchant who had been the power behind Bradford City ever since the club had been formed before the First World War.

James met Paton through his friend Jock Ewert: 'I went over with Jock Ewert to see his old team, Bradford City, play Rochdale. Mr X was there and we became friends right from our first introduction.'

Paton had joined the Bradford City board in 1906, though he had been involved in the club's formation some three years earlier. He saw Bradford gain promotion to the First Division in 1908, and take the FA Cup in 1911, before he stepped down, and he remained an influential figure behind the scenes.

In the late 1920s, Bradford began to struggle; it was relegated to the Third Division North in 1927, support dropped and the club came close to liquidation. Paton engineered a boardroom revolution, dispensing with all the old directors and installing his own men. He backed up this move with a large amount of cash and he swiftly pulled the club round. It gained promotion in 1928/29, after which Paton once again stepped out of the limelight.

Herbert Chapman acknowledged Paton's influence in 1932: 'He was the power behind the club and it was largely through the energy that he threw into the task that promotion was achieved. During that season, Bradford's gates were almost doubled.'

Chapman was a close friend of Paton's, having spent many years in the Huddersfield–Leeds–Bradford area; he admired Paton's drive and, possibly, his power.

Sam Barkus, then a young player at Bradford City, recalled Paton and his generosity:

> He often gave me a £5 note. He was able to buy people – he bought Bradford City back into the Second Division, there's no doubt about that. I remember having a drink with a South Shields player, Turnbull, one evening and we recalled a 3-1 win Bradford had scored over Shields. Turnbull said to me, 'Aye, I had £10 out of that!' Paton had paid some of the South Shields players to lose! He was a very wealthy man, a wool merchant, and he carried a wool travelling rug around with him. He brought people down from Scotland who would do as he told, like the manager O'Rourke – a Lanarkshire man. He knew what Paton wanted, knew his methods.

Paton immediately appealed to Alex James (powerful, rich, self-made men usually did) and in the summer of 1929, with James becalmed – Preston away on a tour of the United States and no transfer deal signed – he went to Paton's home on the Ayrshire coast for a short holiday. On the links at Turnberry, Paton promised to help James if he could.

Later that summer, back in Nottingham with the family staying with his in-laws, James received a telegram from Mr X: 'Meet me at so-and-so, in Bradford,' it read.

> I packed at once and caught the first available train north. When I reached Bradford I made a quick dash round to the place where I had fixed to meet Mr X.
>
> He was there. And so, to my amazement, was the great Herbert Chapman, manager of Arsenal. We all sat down for a talk.

It emerged that Chapman had contacted Preston in mid-May; the clubs had agreed a price. It was up to James.

Before James could begin his laboured request for illegal cash, Paton intervened to say that he and Chapman had arranged an alternative way of solving James's 'past difficulties'. Chapman then revealed that a job had been arranged for him outside football. 'You will act as a sports demonstrator at a West End store at a salary of £250 a year, and I have arrange a two-year contract for you.'

The job, Chapman explained, would circumvent the League restriction on 'illegal inducements', as it was the store and not Arsenal who would apparently be offering the job. And there were no rules to prevent a professional player from having more than one job. James was keen on the idea:

> It was just what I wanted. It would give me an insight into up-to-date business methods and when that appointment ended I would be able to go into business myself . . . I was given details of the work and was ready to accept at once. All along I had felt that London was the best place in which I could land, though I had not been able to give voice to my thoughts.

At this point, the diplomatic wiles of Chapman came into play. With the knowledge that the League would certainly want to scrutinize the deal, he took the wind out of their sails by requesting ('in view of the statements made about the player') an enquiry himself.

Taking the precaution of obtaining James's signature first (while on another weekend golfing holiday at Turnberry) Chapman laid out the deal for the League officials to study.

After hearing evidence from the various unsuccessful clubs, none of whom had anything incriminating to say, the League committee had to decide first whether Arsenal had been responsible for the sports demonstrator's appointment, second if it was a *bona fide* appointment and lastly if the player was capable of filling it. Though they were unprepared to give Arsenal a completely clean bill of health, they eventually decided that nothing should stand in the way of the deal. They were unhappy, they declared, 'with certain things that had been said', though they made it plain they were not complaining about anything Taylor or Preston had done. They simply smelled a rat, but could prove nothing.

'The way is free' Ivan Sharpe wrote in *Athletic News* the following Monday, 'for James to join Arsenal as, of course, he is willing to do provided his weekend consultation with an adviser from his native country, whose home is in the North of England, does not produce a hitch.'

There were, of course, no hitches. How could there be? Paton, with his close business arrangements with the top London store, had arranged the job himself. In fact, it had been the sports demon-strator's job at Selfridges that James had agreed to first; Arsenal had almost been secondary.

In Preston, just as at Kirkcaldy, the feeling among the supporters was of an almost personal loss. James, like all great players, had made the fortnightly tramp to Deepdale in the rain and cold worth every penny. Without him, the reality of Preston's plight could no longer be ignored.

'To me, and thousands of others, his going is a sort of football tragedy,' commented 'Perseus' in the *Lancashire Daily Post*. To say he would not be missed, he added, was to lose all sense of football's values.

James himself, in a parting interview, was diplomatic: he didn't want to leave Preston, he said. 'I like the town, and I like the people, but I have to do the best for masel'.'

12

Tactical Tangles

On the eve of the final, in a long talk in London that I had with him, Mr Chapman told me that there was only one place for James and that is London. Only one club in London for him, and that was the Arsenal.

Lancashire Daily Post, May 1929

CHAPMAN WAS CERTAINLY correct about London. Even in 1930, with the great Crash still reverberating around the world and the Depression starting to bite, the south of England, with the greater adaptability of its consumer and service industries, was already pointing the way to economic recovery. The building boom had begun; suburbs were already springing up along the newly extended tube lines.

Already the south was taking on the appearance J. B. Priestly described:

of filling stations and factories that looked like exhibition buildings, of giant cinemas and dance halls and cafes, bungalows with tiny garages, cocktail bars, Woolworths, motor coaches, wirelesses, hiking, factory-girls looking like actresses, greyhound racing and dirt-tracks, swimming pools and everything given away with cigarette coupons.

It was into this new land that James would take his family: out of the terraces of Preston, far from the railway tenement in Mossend, into a semi-detached house with a 'stucco front, creosoted gate, a privet hedge and a green front door . . .'. Here among the technocrats of modern civilisation, the mechanics, airmen, radio experts, film producers, popular journalists and industrial chemists, here he would settle down, never more to roam.

Whether Arsenal was the only club was more questionable. The

TOPICAL TIMES
FOOTBALL ANNUAL

1929
1930

PRICE
3
PENCE⁹

ALEC JAMES

Arsenal James was joining in 1929 could best be summed up by the fact that the tube station opposite the entrance to the ground was still called Gillespie Road rather than Arsenal. There was no grand palatial stand, no marble halls nor commissionaires, no Clock, and the North Bank was still called the Laundry End.

As for achievements – in the League the club had managed just one runners-up position in 1927, but the Spurs of Grimsdell and Dimmock and Seed had managed that in 1921/22. Arsenal had reached the Cup Final in 1927, but, then, so had West Ham in 1923 and Chelsea in 1915, while Spurs could boast two Cup wins – in 1901 and 1921.

Since Chapman had arrived in 1925 Arsenal had been noted more for its high spending and the scandal over Norris than for achievements on the pitch. The Norris trouble had hung like a cloud over Arsenal for two to three years and, it was claimed, had set back the progress Chapman had been making. Certainly, since the near misses in Cup and League in 1926 and 1927, the club had little to show for all the expensive signings.

Fortunately, Spurs had been relegated during this time and thus the pressure upon Chapman had been less intense. Fortunate, too, that Chapman had warned supporters and directors on his arrival that it would be five years before the club won anything.

Had he a five-year plan? Possibly not, although with Herbert Chapman who could say? Planning as an idea and on a grand scale was increasingly the vogue in the late Twenties. The image, if not the method, of Stalin's Russia was at its most seductive, lending prestige to the planning concept; Mussolini had demonstrated how society might be organised and progress plotted with goals and targets for people to aim at.

Chapman had had experience in larger scale man-management in industry, of course, as a manager-in-chief of a munitions factory during the war with a score of sub-managers beneath him. The regimentation, the prescribed targets for production (met in full, and more, by Chapman) the imperatives of war-time, had all impressed upon Chapman the desirability and the advantages of discipline, and of the total centralised control that planning requires.

However, industry released from wartime controls was proving a totally different proposition; the old inefficiencies, the lack of common purpose (exacerbated by class divisions), the tendency to rely on old, obsolete methods and machinery played a major part in Britain's economic collapse. To some acute observers in the late 1920s, football thinking was just as out of date and moribund: 'Perseus' in the *Lancashire Daily Post* wrote in August 1928, in a preview of the next season:

Most clubs will go along the old lines, self-satisfied, hoping for the best but doing little to encourage it, hugging the belief that they are good enough to give the other fellow a licking but not sufficiently keen to study the way to do it most effectively.

And he added, ruefully, 'as far as one can judge, there has been the advent of no football Mussolini, a man capable of evolving new team methods or of giving points to old ones'.

In that, 'Perseus' was wrong. Chapman had been considering 'new' methods and demonstrating a desire to think about tactics ever since he and Charles Buchan had arrived at Arsenal in 1925. Buchan actually claimed in later years to have advocated the defensive centre-half system in a pre-match talk before the kick-off on the first day of the 1925/26 season. The match had been against Tottenham and Arsenal had lost 1-0, Buchan's idea having apparently been rejected.

In fact, Tottenham had 'planned' their tactics, too, ostensibly to counter the threat posed by the high-scoring Buchan. Jimmy Seed, the inside right for Tottenham explained.

I was a member of the Tottenham team that met Arsenal at Highbury in the opening fixture of the 1925/26 season. When I tell you that Charlie Buchan had been one of the stars of the Sunderland team when I had been just a 'colt' on the Roker Park staff, you will realise why I looked forward so much to that game. Buchan was one of my youthful football idols.

Soon after the game commenced, I quickly realised that the dropping back of the centre-half into a purely defensive role had left a wide-open space in the middle of the field. I saw the necessity for some member of the team to fill that gap or, at least, to cover it up, so I dropped back behind the other forwards in order to pick up any loose balls that might be lying around in open spaces.

Although I didn't appreciate it at the time, I had accidentally hit upon the effective counter to the revised offside ruling, the roving forward playing behind the other attackers as a sort of centre-half-cum-forward.

I don't wish to take any credit for the move I made because I had never even considered the adoption of the method before I stepped on to the field at Highbury that afternoon. It was quite automatic and performed on the spur of the moment.

So much, he appears to be saying, for all those much-vaunted pre-match talks! Buchan, meanwhile, carried on arguing – in vain – for the new method well into November, when a 7-0 thrashing by Newcastle persuaded Chapman to give the idea a try.

Buchan fancied the Seed midfield role himself, a case of the master copying the pupil. But Chapman insisted that Buchan had been bought to score goals and so the privilege of becoming Arsenal's first 'roving' schemer settled at first upon one Andy Neil, then a third-team player. Chapman is supposed to have said, 'He's as slow as a funeral but has ball control and can stand on the ball while making up his mind!'

In the following seasons, however, the position remained undefined and unfilled by anyone of great talent, during which time Arsenal rose no higher than ninth in the First Division.

Meanwhile, Jimmy Seed had moved on to Sheffield Wednesday and, as captain and creator-in-chief, led the Owls to two championship titles in a row in 1929 and 1930 and it is clear that Chapman was searching throughout this period for just such an influential player.

When he bought Alex James, he knew he had at last secured a man able to build attacks and release forward players, an accurate passer and 'reader' of the game who could switch the focus of the attack when desired. For more than a year he had watched him playing for Preston and Scotland, and had seen how James quite naturally dropped back, at times almost into the half-back line.

James was 27 years old when he arrived at Highbury. He was at the peak of his playing powers, full of confidence and sure of the strengths of his game. Whether Herbert Chapman was sure about the strengths of his team is less certain.

Arsenal began well with four wins in five games but from 21 September until 19 February managed only five more wins; during this time they lost 11 games and drew five. They were thus closer to relegation than to the Championship.

Chapman was desperately ringing the changes throughout: in the first 14 games of the season he used 12 different forwards, involving 20 different positional changes, but things continued to go from bad to worse. Those first 14 games produced seven wins and 16 points; the next 14 games produced four wins and eight defeats. In November, when the crisis was at its height, Chapman plunged into the transfer market and bought Dave Halliday to replace centre-forward Ted Lambert. But Ted Lambert was not the problem. Neither was Alex James. Yet it was James who was taking the brunt of the criticism.

James certainly appeared to be all at sea in the Arsenal set-up,

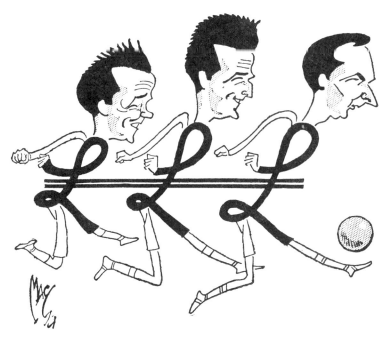

Our artist's impression of Arsenal's trio of high-priced inside forwards—James, Halliday and Jack.

playing poorly and ineffectually. The crowd had turned against him with a vengeance and the newspaper critics were scathing:

> The James plan of holding a roving commission betwixt halves and forwards may have its points. What was not open to debate on Saturday was that the little man was too prone to keep the ball to himself until he was beaten by force of numbers. He would do well to remember there are four other forwards in the side.
>
> *Daily Mail,* October 1929

Yet how could a player like James, bought for a specific job, one that he had been performing so effectively at Preston, be failing so comprehensively?

The problem was threefold. First, the Arsenal tactical system that would soon be sweeping all before it was still in a state of flux, only partly thought through; second, James was a complicated player at the best of times, difficult for other players to 'read'; and third, James was seriously unfit.

Tactically, Chapman had perfected only one half of his

'machine': the defence. Yet its success was creating difficulties for the rest of the team, and for James in particular. The intricate system of covering and shepherding of opponents involved the Arsenal defence in retreating, giving ground to opponents, luring them into losing the ball. Turning possession into effective attack was thus a problem because possession was often achieved when the 'creator' – James – was deep in his own half, having fallen back with the defence.

The conventional wisdom that he was unwilling to do defensive work was wide of the mark. Alex Jackson was certain James was under-rated as a defender:

> His strength in the tackle has to be experienced to be understood. Being short in the leg and heavy for his height, he is a more difficult man to move once he gets his foot on the ball. He does a great deal of defensive work without touching the ball, merely by forcing an opponent to part with it.
>
> *Glasgow Evening Times,* November 1931

James was carrying out his defensive duties, all right, but drawn back much deeper than he had anticipated. And it was clear he disagreed with Chapman over exactly how much could be achieved from such a position. He wrote in the *Star* a year later,

> The First Division inside forward cannot possibly do all that is expected of him, i.e. donkey work, fetching and carrying, initiating all attacks, falling back and defending. Being human, and not a whirlwind, I say frankly that it cannot be done.

Chapman's work was far from over, therefore. The system needed something extra.

Where James's own methods were concerned, and his colleagues' adjustment to them, the problem was of a long-term nature:

James always claimed that he held on to the ball and dribbled with it for one reason alone: to create space and to draw defenders towards him, thus releasing colleagues further forward. Holding the ball was a painful business in first-class football: 'The player who dribbles unnecessarily is asked for trouble and deserves it.' Thus, the only time he was caught in possession was when there was no one to pass to. It was useless to give it to someone who was poorly positioned: 'He will only lose the ball so you might as well do that yourself.'

He was also very clear about what he expected his colleagues to do when they got possession of the ball. In the same article he wrote:

I always try to get somewhere clear of the opposition so that my colleagues are able to pass to me without interference. If they fail to do so, that's their funeral, not mine. I consider I have done my part of the job by getting into position.

Coming to terms with a player with such a quicksilver mind, with such unorthodox methods, was always going to be difficult for the Arsenal players; even when the team was working smoothly, years later, James would still be a puzzle to them, constantly coming up with ruses and moves that startled them.

James might have made more of a success of his predicament, however, if he had not been playing under a considerable personal handicap, one that became apparent at the very start of his first season at Highbury:

My troubles started almost as soon as I had signed on. After I had arranged for a house in north London, I returned to Preston to see about shifting.

My spare time was spent on the golf-course. Usually when fit I could have gone on playing all day. But now I found my ankle giving out. It was all swollen and a mass of bruises – a legacy of Second Division football.

Now that had been usual for me a week or two at the end of the season and I never worried. For I found that with heavy massaging the ankles recovered in plenty of time for the next campaign. A little of this treatment, I thought, would put me right. Instead, I grew worse and worse. So much so that I had to give up golf. I couldn't last out six holes. The pain was unbearable. At night I was getting no sleep.

He travelled up to Edinburgh to see a specialist, who doubted if he could start the new season. He took treatment and then returned to London and to Arsenal trainer Tom Whittaker.

I well remember my first examination by Tom. He spent some
hours over me, hardly asked a question. The sight of my swollen
ankle, however, had given him a big shock.
    When he was finished with me he went in to see Mr Chapman.
'You've signed an out-and-out crock' was the gist of his report.
And it certainly seemed like it.

It was a difficult moment for James when Chapman heard
Whittaker's report:

I felt it badly. You see, I had never mentioned it much to Mr
Chapman. When he signed me on I was far too concerned with
the enquiry to pay any real attention to my injuries ... I told him
frankly I was not fit but said I would be all right as soon as I got
out on the field with the boys.

And so he played in the first game against Leeds: 'Every movement
was an effort and I simply couldn't get going. Add to that the fact
that I was strange to the team and it would have been surprising had
I made a hit in the first game.'
    Towards the end of the game, he caught his ankle in a divot hole
and made the injury worse. The following week, against Manchester City, he was injured again and the *Daily Mail* reported that he
had returned with his foot in bandages. He missed the next two
games.

My legs got worse. I had no chance to rest them ... every spare
minute of my time was taken up in massage – the only cure for
my troubles apart from a prolonged rest in bed. My nose and
stomach were troubling me and needed urgent attention.
Altogether, I was a pretty fine wreck.

It had taken Tom Whittaker, the club physiotherapist, some time to
work James's problems out:

Alex was one of the most amazing 'clients' I had on my hands
in the dressing-room. When he first arrived at Highbury and came
in for treatment I used to think he was playing the 'old soldier'.
Although he used to complain of bruises on his legs I could not
find any. And even when I had seen for myself the treatment the

'the most kicked man in soccer' got on the field, I still could not find any bruises. So I figured there was either something wrong with his legs or that he had peculiar skin and muscle formation that never showed a mark even if hit with a hammer. But the very dark skin of Alex's shins contrasting to the colour of the rest of his legs gave the clue. Alex had so many deep-seated bruises that the whole of both shins from stocking top to ankle were almost mahogany in colour! So I set to work patiently to eradicate the previous injuries . . . but he was such a great-hearted little man that he would play on and on when other men would demand a rest owing to the pain in their legs.

The crowd at Arsenal, of course, knew nothing of James's injuries and were prepared to make no allowances. Chapman was outraged by their treatment of James:

I shall always think the dead set which was made against him was deliberately manufactured to hurt the club as well as the player. It was one of the meanest things I have ever known and one of the finest players it has been my pleasure to see almost had his heart broken. That is not an exaggeration.

James tried to laugh it off:

Every day when I went down to the ground for training there would be a pile of letters waiting for me. Practically all in the same strain. Advising me to go back to Scotland or stand down or give a better man a chance and so on.

I recall that the day we played Newcastle United at home a neat little parcel arrived for me when we were stripping. It was nicely sealed and I wondered whether I would open it or wait till the end of the game.

In the end, I opened it. Inside was a pair of kid's football boots, very old and battered. And, of course, a covering letter. 'You might try these boots,' it ran, 'as it doesn't matter much what you wear anyhow,' etc., etc.

I had a good laugh and then passed the letter round.

Thomson's Weekly News, 31 June 1931

James had been warned of the intolerance of certain sections of the

Highbury crowd. David Jack, who had cost the club £10,000 the previous season, had also been subjected to abuse and criticism when he had struggled to find form early on. With the arrival of James, Jack looked forward to the burden being lifted from his shoulders:

> Quite by chance, I met Alec at Kemptown Racecourse in the close season shortly after it was known that he would be playing at Highbury the following season.
> Preliminary greetings over, as I shook his hand on leaving I said, 'Well Alec, your football education is just beginning.'
> I left him to think that one over for himself'
> *Thomson's Weekly News*, August 1934

The crisis point for James and Arsenal was reached in the New Year. After a terrible performance against Sheffield Wednesday he was dropped. It was a week before Arsenal's first Cup match of the season against local rivals, Chelsea. He was asked if thought he would be fit – he said no.

> It was suggested that the press should be informed that I was only dropped because of injury,
> 'If I'm dropped, say I'm dropped,' was my reply to that. What's the use of beating about the bush? Mind you, I was unfit. But no more so than during the previous months when I had played.

Arsenal won the Cup match 2-0, and the following day the club's physician ordered James to bed for a couple of weeks. 'I never knew how bad I was until that period in bed. Sleep was a stranger to me and to make the pain bearable, I had to have injections.'
In the next round of the Cup, Arsenal drew with Birmingham at home. James listened in on radio at home but, the following morning, Herbert Chapman appeared at the James home.

> 'Come on,' he said, 'on with your clothes and come to Brighton with the boys.'
> 'What for?' I said.
> 'Why, for the replay at Birmingham. You're going to win the match for us.'

The manner of his approach concealed a genuine perplexity on Chapman's behalf. As he later admitted, '. . . I did not know how we were going to get him back into the side.'

And James later claimed that it had been Phil Kelso, a manager and friend of James's, who had rung Chapman up and told him that his best chance of winning the replay was to get James out of bed.

Whatever the origin of the decision, the gamble paid off. James was no fitter; in fact, he confessed to finding it difficult just to kick the ball. But the Birmingham players did not know that:

> When I took the field at Birmingham I was laughing to myself at all the stuff that had been written about my selection. For it was generally held that I might prove a match-winning factor . . . I honestly didn't know whether I was standing on my head or my heels.

Arsenal won a dour match 1-0, a penalty dividing the two teams. In the dressing-room afterwards, team-mates crowded round him to congratulate him on his display: 'It was another heartening stunt on the part of my colleagues . . . they knew as well as I did that I hadn't done a thing . . .'

But Chapman *had* done something and, in a sense, he had unlocked his own system.

James's assertion that he could not do all that was apparently demanded of him was quite true. His new role, falling back with a retreating defence, left the forward line a man short for most of the time. Wingers cutting in had been part of the new tactical formation but Chapman realised that he needed someone, particularly on the left, to take on both left-sided forward positions when the team was on the attack.

Cliff Bastin, the missing piece in the jigsaw, was only approached by Chapman in December 1929 and told that he should move to outside left (he had originally been bought as an inside forward). The switch came as something of a shock to Bastin, who needed some persuading – but that was Chapman's forte, convincing men that they could do whatever it was he wanted them to.

Thus, in a confusing and chaotic moment, was the famous James-Bastin partnership born. In fact, they were to play together only once in 1929, on 26 December. James was to miss four of the next five games, returning to the team for the Cup replay on 29 January.

After that, the two played together as a wing partnership for 16 more games, though it was not until 15 February that Bastin scored his first goal with James alongside him.

James later claimed that many of Arsenal's troubles were due to the fact that no one understood his methods: 'And now that we all work together smoothly I'm told how well I'm playing compared with those first few months. Frankly, that defeats me. I've never altered my style one bit since I arrived at Highbury.'

That may not have been completely true; he certainly adjusted his skills to those around and in front of him once he saw how fast and effective those men could be.

But the idea that Chapman somehow 'moulded' James into some preconceived 'roving commissioner' must also be seen as wide of the mark. Chapman was a great adapter: he is credited with having created a system and fitted it to match and enhance the skills of the men he had on hand, not vice versa. His successful transplantation of James at the heart of the Arsenal side (after a potentially disastrous rejection) was undoubtedly a triumph.

It was Alex James's triumph, however, that he turned Chapman's essentially defensive system of play into something more exciting and scintillating than it might otherwise have been. For once James achieved full fitness, his multiple talents were to blossom in the new formation as they had never done before. The only aspect of his game that was to be submerged was his ability to score spectacular goals, the sort that he had made his trademark at Raith and Preston.

In early 1930, as the Cup continued, League form gradually revived. The side battled their way past Middlesbrough, West Ham and, in the semi-final, Hull City, the Second Division side having taken Arsenal to a replay in a rough, bruising encounter in which they had led 2-0 in the first half.

Against Middlesbrough, James had shown flashes of the form that would become commonplace in the season to come:

When Arsenal scored their first goal it looked as if James had delayed his pass too long. He dribbled over to the right and, having taken the Middlesbrough defenders with him, he suddenly drew the ball back, turned and pushed it down the middle. It was a masterly effort and Lambert only had to place his shot carefully to be certain of scoring. *Daily Mail*, February 1930.

13

King James

A TRIUMPH OF TACTICS

I can recall no man who has ever come out of a Cup Final with so many honours as James. Surely he has at last justified himself and, as one of those who
has persistently proclaimed him in the face of the sternest criticism as the
cleverest inside forward since the reign of Bobby Walker, his outstanding
brilliance was very pleasing to me.   'Arbiter' in the *Daily Mail*, 1930

ON CUP FINAL day it is rare for the expected star to shine, perhaps
because Cup Finals have about them an unreal nightmarish quality
which only the truly nerveless can ignore; those men blissfully
immune to the voodoo magic conjured up by the rituals, the super-
stitions and the strange feeling that the whole nation has its eyes
fixed squarely upon the rectangular piece of Wembley turf.

A few days before the Cup Final, James professed to be unmoved
by it all: 'I never worry about any match,' he told readers of the
Daily Express. 'I am not given to excitement either on or off the
field.'

And yet, he had to admit once it was all over that, 'It was glorious and pulsating from start to finish – an entirely different atmosphere from that of two internationals in which I have participated
at Wembley . . .'

As a Scot, he could be forgiven for underestimating the power of
the occasion. For the English, insular as ever, the Cup Final stands
supreme as the climax to the season, while north of the border *the*
match – be it home or away – is the England–Scotland international.

Thus, for James, the Wembley match that had mattered most had
ended, three weeks previously, in shattering defeat. Two years after
being defeated by the Wembley Wizards, England had almost exactly turned the tables with a 5-2 victory.

In a season of turmoil and trouble, the Wembley defeat must have
been a bitter pill for James to swallow. For the first time in seven

appearances for Scotland he had been on the losing side and, after two victories over the Old Enemy, defeat had come in such a way as to cast yet more doubt upon his talents and ability.

The previous season in 1929, with the Hampden crowd primed and ready to acknowledge their Wembley Wizards in yet another crushing defeat of the English, the team as a whole had failed. On a fast ground, in blazing sunshine and a swirling wind, victory had been achieved with a freak goal scored from a corner. Only James had reproduced the expected form:

'James was the one man who rose above the conditions and his ball control was almost uncanny,' wrote Bob McColl, while 'Clutha' in the *Glasgow Evening Times* wrote: 'The great forward of the game was assuredly James. Scotland may have had his equal but never his superior.'

But in 1930 at Wembley, as England dashed to a 4-0 lead in the first half, Alex James's international world was falling apart.

The portents had always looked bad. Until 1930 there had been a comforting familiarity about the team whenever James had played: Jimmy McMullen had been behind him at left half, Alan Morton on his immediate left, Hughie Gallacher to his right at centre-forward with Alex Jackson away on the right wing. Jimmy Gibson had also been a regular in the half-back line.

But 1930 saw McMullen bow out of international football, Craig of Rangers taking his place. For Wembley, Gallacher had cried off in order to help Newcastle avoid relegation and Jimmy Gibson was injured. What's more, James had been moved from inside left:

Geordie Stevenson of Motherwell had partnered Alex Jackson against Ireland but we were changed over for the Wembley game. Inside left was his natural position and I understand it was felt I would adjust myself to the right wing easier. It was meant as a compliment but I don't think it was realised I had played there only once in three years.

From Scotland's point of view, however, the team was considered a well-balanced one and, gratifying to the 'purists', almost exclusively made up from 'home' Scots: six from Rangers, one from Hearts and Motherwell. Only James (Arsenal) Jackson (Huddersfield) and Law (Chelsea) were 'Anglos' – an exact reversal of the Wizards.

England, meanwhile, based their team around the League Champions, Sheffield Wednesday, and challengers Derby; Sheffield supplied four men, and the brilliant right-winger Crooks came from Derby. Thus it was almost a League battle, and the English victory was attributed to just such a clash in styles. As a Scots commentator grudgingly conceded: 'English methods prevailed as they will occasionally do against craft and science. England darted where Scotland dawdled, pounded where Scotland poised.'

Though the victory had apparently been such a crushing one, any Englishman naive enough to claim that the Wizards' defeat had been avenged was soon disabused. 'Clutha', in the *Glasgow Evening Times*, claimed that there had been cheers in Glasgow when the result came through – cheers of relief, that is, because though they had been defeated, they had not been disgraced!

Be that as it may, James's career seemed in jeopardy. Though most reporters considered him the least culpable of the forward line, he himself knew he had played badly:

> Alex Jackson and I are great pals but I didn't feel at home as his partner. I had got into the way of swinging the ball out to him from the left-wing position to give him a clear run through. Playing so close to him cramped my style somewhat.

There was also a body of opinion north of the border that did not regard him as an international player. A Scots journalist wrote:

> I have always held that James was a brilliant juggler with the ball but too much of an individualist in an international side . . . An international eleven is a thing of a day; combination must be struck in a moment if success is to be attained. Thus, in my view, it is always desirable to play the combining type of forward in the inside positions. James may be as clever as they make 'em, but he is not this . . .

Add to that the growing certainty that international elevens would soon be selected from home-based players only, and his Scottish international days would appear to be numbered. And for James that was serious.

The Scottish team that he had appeared in just three weeks before the Cup Final had been the basis for his claim to fame. By the end of 1930, he would have played in seven international games and been on the winning side six times in a row. He would have scored four goals in those seven games – the side as a whole would have scored 25 and they would have beaten England 5-1 and Ireland 7-3. His career with Raith, Preston and Arsenal had produced nothing to match it.

Thus, the Cup Final came at a moment in his career when his future as a star player was very much at stake, when everything he had hoped for – not least the cherished 'business opportunities' – hung precariously in the balance.

I often wonder, [he wrote some years later] what Herbert Chapman would have done at the end of the season if we had not won the cup. Chapman was never a man to give two thoughts to the fact that a player had cost many thousands of £'s to buy.

If he did not make good, well, he was no use to Arsenal and would have to go. They had paid £9,000 for me but, I tell you quite frankly, that if we hadn't won at Wembley, I am fairly certain in my own mind that Alex James would have been up for sale again.

So much at stake, and so much depending on a side that James confessed later to thinking was the worst side he was to play in during his eight years at Highbury.

If that sounds something of an exaggeration, they were still very much an unknown quantity: a mixture of veterans such as Tom Parker, Bob John and Charlie Jones, plus untested youngsters like Cliff Bastin (17 years old) and Eddie Hapgood. David Jack was carrying an injury that would reduce him to a passenger in the second half. Preedy was a goalkeeper in whom even his friends had little faith. And then there was James himself, who had struggled through a season of pain and controversy and still had not justified, in the eyes of many, his huge transfer fee.

And up against them: a Huddersfield Town side whose club pedigree was unequalled since the War. A hat trick of championships, twice runners-up, three times Cup Finalists and staffed by a host of English internationals: Goodall at right back, Wilson at centre-half, Kelly at inside right, Smith on the left wing . . . the team Chapman had created and which many felt he could never hope to emulate.

Hugh Gallacher

Alex James

Tom Jennings

Dave Morris

Alex Jackson

Bob John

Eddie Hapgood

Cliff Bastin

Ted Drake

Cigarette cards immortalised famous players, though without rewarding them in any other way

April 1932; in a match against West Ham, James was carried off unconscious with a knee injury which led to his missing the Cup Final. (Illustrated London News)

December 1932; James is back to fitness, and tests the Gymno-Frame, a muscle developer made of tensile steel tubes in the Highbury gym. (BBC Hulton Picture Library)

Though only five of the Huddersfield Cup side of 1928 lined up to face Arsenal, it now included Alex Jackson, possibly the League's most exciting right-winger after the Englishman Sammy Crooks; and it had a new international star at left half in Campbell, who already possessed a Cup-winner's medal for Blackburn.

But the Huddersfield Town side was also vulnerable: it relied too much on Jackson and it was gambling on a centre-forward who, one critic declared, 'is more or less a lottery in the position.'

Predicting the result was, therefore, also something of a lottery: would Bastin cope? Was Jack fit? Would Jackson triumph? Would Preedy do something impetuous?

And, hovering over everything, just as the Graf Zeppelin would momentarily do during the game, was the imposing figure of Herbert Chapman who knew both teams and most of the players better than they knew themselves.

The day of the Final was clear and bright. Arsenal lost the toss and were assigned to the 'unlucky' dressing-room but, '. . . away went the Arsenal to banish all superstition and, to help them, a gramophone played lively airs while they dressed. This was Mr Chapman's idea . . .'

And so, to the strains of Harry Roy, Ambrose and Al Jolson, the Arsenal team dressed, confident and, as Chapman put it, 'Carnera fit'.

Outside, Scottish observers were casting a superior eye over this most English of occasions:

On the way to the scene of the conflict I met a flaming procession consisting of an Arsenal fan and friends covered in red from head to foot and carrying a copy of the Cup in the same colour and half a hundred followers all similarly attired.

Glasgow Evening News

Another reporter could not help wondering why a group of Arsenal supporters started singing 'The Bonnie Banks of Loch Lomond' as he passed by into the stadium. 'They may have heard Alex James singing it sometimes' he mused. Inside the stadium, 'all sorts of aural torture were in evidence – all the things taboo in Glasgow such as bugles, bells, rickety-racketees and mascots of every conceivable shape . . .'

And yet he was impressed by the pageantry and the singing: 'The hymn "Abide With Me" and the National Anthem really are vastly preferably to "The Wells o' Weary" and other less desirable rubbish wafted up to the press box on some of our big days—'

As the teams lined up, Scotland was still very much on his mind: 'Arsenal, with their post-office red shirts, reminded me of the Forfarshire "Red Lichties". . . Huddersfield in heavy vertical stripes made one think of St Mirren—'

The match kicked off in bright sunshine and, within minutes, Arsenal was pressing in on Huddersfield's goal. A free kick for hands by Wilson for Huddersfield on the edge of the area was awarded:

> James prepared to take this, calmly called for referee Crew to insist on the stipulated distance being observed between the ball and his opponents, then suddenly made himself scarce, leaving Tom Parker to bash the ball. It was a cute ruse but it didn't come off.

Then James put Lambert through down the middle but the Huddersfield keeper deflected the ball for a corner. There followed more near misses, Bastin and Lambert heading wide or just over until, in the tenth minute, Smith broke away down the left, beat Baker and Parker, and centred. Jackson came dashing in but his full-length diving header went wide.

Arsenal, however, were in control and James was at the heart of everything the team did:

> For sheer, saucy audacity he cannot be beaten. Meandering down the middle, steering to the left or else darting to the right it was the same – he invariably knew the right road and his opponents had gone the other one.

With 15 minutes gone, James produced a masterstroke. Goodall had fouled him outside the area:

> Quick as lightning – I didn't hear the referee's signal for the free kick to be taken – James pushed the ball forward to Bastin. The wing man ran nearly to the corner-flag and, when challenged by Goodall, doubled back and centred to James who had run forward. James received the pass in his stride and shot a great goal!

James later explained that the move had been discussed with Bastin prior to the match. In an interview with 'Arbiter', of the *Daily Mail* he revealed:

> We arranged that instead of centring I should go close up and he should give me a square pass. It was a beauty which he gave me. The ball came along the ground just at the right pace to let me jump over it as it ran past. If I had stopped it I should have lost the chance. Even then Turner had positioned himself so well that I saw that I could only hope to beat him by some deception. So I sliced the ball with the outside of my right foot and sent it swerving beyond the reach of the goalkeeper's left hand.

The Huddersfield team rushed to protest that the kick had been illegally taken, but the referee disagreed: 'I did not whistle; the rule say I must give a signal. I did this by a wave of the hand so there could be no doubt about the genuineness of the goal' (*Courier and Advertiser*, 28 April 1930).

James agreed:

> It was a perfectly good goal, but I was lucky to get away with it that day. In Scotland, as soon as a man is fouled you can take the kick. Provided, of course, you place it correctly and see that it is dead. Usually, a Scots player gives it a little tap to his nearest colleague. The idea, of course, is to make sure the other side gets no chance to recover.
>
> All the time I was with Preston and up to that day at Wembley I had adopted this plan. Nine times out of 10 the kick had to be taken over again.

The irony was that James' persistence in this had been a source of great annoyance to Herbert Chapman:

As Tom Whittaker revealed:

> It is strange that he helped to win the Cup by virtually disobeying an order from his chief. During the season since his arrival at Highbury, Mr Chapman had often shown his irritation and disapproval of Alec's attempts to gain advantage by taking quick free-kicks. Although Alec had found English referees were not 'educated' to this, he still persisted in his habit, much to

CUP HISTORY M

THE JUSTIFICATION OF ALEC JAMES

WEMBLEY
BATTLE
STAR

WIZARDRY
IN THE
CUP FINAL

ALEC JAMES.

Famous Scot Scotches His Critics
BY OUR OWN REPRESENTATIVE.

ARSENAL'

Great Goal

in

CUP WON

HUDDERSF

Defied by R
(SPECIAL R

ALEC JAMES WINS CUP FOR ARSENAL.

MORE WEMBLEY WIZARDRY — A
GOAL AND A HAND IN THE OTHER
—EASILY THE BEST FORWARD ON
THE FIELD — OTHER "STARS"
DIMMED BY COMPARISON.

Tom Parker,
Arsenal.

Tom Wilson,
Huddersfield T.

ENDLESS THRILLS BUT LITTLE HIGH-CLASS FOOTBALL.
By "JACK O' CLUBS."
Arsenal...................................2   Huddersfield Town...............................0

CU

Bri

ARSE

Page

HO

JAMES'S JOY-DAY.

Londoners' Great Defence Defies All Huddersfield's Attacks.

ARSENAL - - - 2   HUDDERSFIELD TOWN - - 0

By THOMAS MOULT.

E AT WEMBLEY

IG JAMES

Great Part

ry

IRST TIME

UNLUCKY

Goalkeeper

EXPERTS)

THE F.A. CUP GOES TO LONDON

JAMES THE MAN WHO MATTERED

His Great Display and First Goal—
Lambert Puts on Finishing Touch—
Huddersfield Town Out of Luck.

Arsenal - - - 2 Huddersfield Town - 0
James, Lambert.   Half-time: 1-0.
AT WEMBLEY STADIUM.

By BILLY MEREDITH.

James scored the first goal at Wembley.

UMPH OF ARSENAL'S

)LDEN" FORWARDS

dersfield Fails: Final	Great Day for James and An Amazingly Lucky One For Preedy

By Harold Kendrick ("Syrian")

mbert) . . 2   HUDDERSFIELD 0

JAMES REPLIES TO HIS CRITICS.

Bull's-Eye Bang Lands Cup.

ENAL TRIUMPHED IN THE CUP FINAL

James the Inspiring Genius of the Match: Second Half Tactics which Nearly Let Huddersfield in: Lambert's Great Goal

ARSENAL 2   HUDDERSFIELD TOWN 0
(James, Lambert.)

Chapman's annoyance. It was not that the Boss objected to the
ethics of the move but that he was annoyed by the fact that Alec
would not see reason . . .

Ironic, too, that despite all the talk about plans and team talks, it
was a flash of inspiration combined with a quiet word with Bastin
on the team bus on the way to the game that had broken the
deadlock. 'You can imagine the inquest which Chapman held in the
dressing room after the game – and the delight of Alec in telling
him just what happened!'
From then on, Arsenal had their work cut out to preserve their
lead. In the second half, Huddersfield pressed relentlessly forward
and Jack Point described how Arsenal were forced to defend for
long periods:

> At this stage James was a semi-half back, and needed as such.
> Huddersfield had been hammering at the Arsenal door and an
> explosion was only averted by safety means.
> Somehow, Arsenal's forwards had faded out of the game.
> David Jack was often on the turf. He went down easily, it seemed,
> and James was often back helping a defence harassed beyond
> endurance. How they kept their end up was nothing short of
> remarkable . . . they were in desperate straits. But it all worked
> out in the end. Alec James took over the duties of pilot, chief
> engineer and Lord High Everything Else – a veritable Pooh Bah.

There were many sterling performances in the Arsenal team that
afternoon. Bob John and Eddie Hapgood effectively nullified much
of what Alex Jackson tried to do, though in the opinion of 'Captain
Bob' in the Scottish *Sunday Post,* they did it illegally: 'I have never
seen a man so badly fouled and so frequently as was Alex Jackson
. . .'; Seddon played the 'stopper' centre-half role to perfection;
Bastin, while not a dominating force, had tussled effectively with
the experienced Goodall; even Preedy, the Arsenal goalkeeper,
despite making wild dashes to the edge of the penalty area ('What
a foolish thing for a goalkeeper to do!' commented referee J. T.
Howcraft afterwards) somehow managed to do just what he had
promised to do on the coach travelling to the ground when he had
stood up and said: 'Boys, I know you think I'm the worst goalkeeper

in the world. I probably am, but today I'm going to play like the best. Nothing is going to get past Charlie Preedy this afternoon.'

Dominating everything, though, was Alex James.

It is not exaggerating the situation to say that the multitude generally speaking were never so delighted as when the Arsenal Scot had the ball delivered to his toe.

None had the slightest conception of what he would do. Even when he did the orthodox they were surprised, simply because they began to believe he would never do the orthodox. Note the sequence. It was James who helped the back division of the Arsenal, also the half-backs; it was James who finally wandered to the centre-half position and made one of his telling passes right up the field to get the Huddersfield keeper out of his goal and the defence all spread-eagled so that Lambert could score one more soft Wembley goal.

The second goal had come with just seven minutes to go:

James held the ball long enough to make the halves and backs uncertain of his intentions. Then he pushed the ball straight down the middle where Lambert, between the two backs, could not be challenged promptly by either. Lambert let the ball run past him – saving a second in time – waited until Turner was compelled to leave his goal and placed it so gently to his right that it almost seemed a mockery. Then Lambert turned and clapped his hands, clapped them at James, the arch-schemer who had found the way, seven minutes from time, to make Arsenal's position unassailable.   J. H. Freeman, *Daily Mail*

It was, as one newspaper put it, 'James's Joy Day'. It was apt that he should have been the one in possession when the game ended.

As the final minutes ticked away and the cheering of the crowd grew louder and louder I thought I would like to have a souvenir of the occasion.

I had my eye on the ball and, strangely enough, the whistle went while I was dribbling with it. Altogether a very satisfying afternoon's work for me.

He had possessed the ball, the crowd and in the days that followed he possessed the headlines.

Hardly a headline failed to proclaim his triumph:

'James' Sparkling Football. James the Inspiring Genius of the Match' (*Sunday Graphic*); 'Magic Touch of James' (*Daily Mail*); 'Alec James the Wizard' (*Sunday Post*); 'James the Master Player' (*Daily Mail*). Billy Meredith writing for the *Daily Dispatch* declared that his scheming, passing and general cleverness had not been surpassed – he had been 'The Man Who Mattered'. Charles Buchan considered he had been 'The Shining Light of the Attack', while in the *Sunday Chronicle* Harold Kenrick considered that it was 'Difficult to estimate what Arsenal owes to James'.

For the Scots present at Wembley, the result had been a triumph for Scottish technique; much as the English might try and put the victory down to planning, method and tactics, so the Scots writers insisted that James alone had provided the real football on offer.

The majority of Scots commentators, in fact, considered the match overall a poor one from an aesthetic point of view. James agreed: 'I have to confess my disappointment in the general quality of the football displayed.'

'Jack O' Clubs' in the *Sporting Record and Mail* was typical of many. It had, he thought, been a great spectacle. 'Yet compared with the environment and all else the play itself was disappointing to me. I mean disappointing in the sense that the brand of football served up was not top quality.' It had pace and punch and, of course, thrills galore, no standing on ceremony: 'Full-blooded stuff every time.' Arsenal, he thought, had been lucky but had deserved their luck, but barring Alex James, the 'star' men on view were more or less lustreless:

In closing, I would like to emphasise once more that this Cup Final of 1930 will, I think, go down the years as that in which one man, and he the smallest man of the 22, stood head and shoulders above the rest. I take my hat off to Alex James. He was the one bright star.

14

Hitting the Headlines

An Islington man, playfully signing himself Ramsey McDonald, says that I ought to be ashamed of myself for taking £10 a week from Gordon Selfridge whilst he (the writer) could sell more goods than me yet he has been unemployed for three and a half years!

Alex James in the *Daily Sketch*, August 1931

ALEX JAMES HAD come to Arsenal with the express intention of bettering himself financially; the job at Selfridges had been the key to Chapman's successful capture of the little man. James had high hopes that it would unlock a world of golden opportunities.

His salary at Selfridges of £250 a year was good when compared with the £150 a year average for most other non-executive Selfridge employees. He was also required to be in the store for far less than the average 50 hours a week most other staff were required to put in. He had to arrive at about 2p.m. most afternoons and stay until the early evening.

And yet, when he had first signed the contract, he had been under the impression that he would not be required to do more than show his face occasionally:

After I had signed for Arsenal I moved to London and took up my sideline job as a sports demonstrator at the store. I had believed this contract to be merely a convenience – just a blind to the FA so that no questions would be asked about my extra £250 a year. I had a shock.

The job was a whole-time affair. I had to be there in the afternoons and leave at night like any other office clerk. My hand ached with signing autographs all day long and I began to think I had been crazy to take the position.

All of which might have raised a hollow laugh in Bellshill. Yet there *was* much more to such a job than met the eye. Shop hours were long in the interwar period, particularly in the highly competitive West End.

In 1931, Selfridges began to experiment with opening the store until seven at night; there was a trade depression on and every extra hour meant more chance to take money. The staff, however, were paid no more for the extra time: they were expected to work the longer hours out of loyalty to the firm, and they did.

James had joined an institution that was remarkably similar in many ways to Arsenal Football Club. Though established as far back as 1909, the Oxford Street store was still growing when James joined the staff in 1929. 1928 had seen the Oxford Street facade extended to its present length, taking on its uniquely grand and classical style; the newly-designed Roof Garden was re-opened at Whitsun 1929 and the store would not be completely finished until the early 1930s when the streets and buildings behind would be incorporated, and the famous clock – the Queen of Time – installed over the front door.

Arsenal's football ground at Highbury, too, was in the process of being radically rebuilt and restyled during these years. The majestic West Stand was constructed in 1932: 'the most advanced, the most architecturally dazzling grandstand ever built in Britain and the first attempt to translate contemporary form and style into football ground design', according to Simon Inglis. Highbury was unquestionably a product of the Thirties; and, with Selfridges, was a visible evidence of the expansion and profitability of the new service sector of the British economy. The similarities did not end there.

Gordon Selfridge and Herbert Chapman, the men at the hearts of these dynamic institutions, though they came from totally different backgrounds and led completely different personal lives, shared significant personal characteristics and motivations. Both were regarded by their respective employees as near geniuses. Both were innovators in their own fields and both were fired by visions that seemed incongruous considering their respective spheres of operation, retailing and football.

Cliff Bastin said of Chapman: 'There was an aura of greatness about him. He possessed a cheery self-confidence. His powers of inspiration and gift of foresight were his greatest attributes. He should have been Prime Minister', while A. H. Williams, second in command to Selfridge, said of his boss: 'Behind his knowledge and his insight into the public mind was his all-pervasive optimism. It seeped out of his office into every department of the store, inspiring every director, buyer, assistant . . . lift-girl.'

Neither man was known to admonish members of staff in such a way as to damage their self-confidence, and neither was vindictive: they ran their respective buildings like benevolent dictators. Selfridge was known to arrive at seven in the morning and still to be there when the last employee had gone home to bed; Chapman, too, according to Bob Wall, was usually the last man off the premises and no member of staff could leave without having first rung through to check with Chapman that he had no objection.

Selfridge had a free hand, of course, and was able to introduce his innovations and experiments without too much opposition. He introduced exciting new publicity stunts, new ways of presenting goods on display, and a revolutionary staff organisation, though he had the burden of knowing that it was largely his money that was at stake.

Chapman, being ostensibly an employee of Arsenal Football Club, had the harder task all round. Yet through his forceful personality and his achievements he was soon to acquire powers to control almost every aspect of the club's operation; he was a professional in a semi-amateur's world, and realised that his job was one that should embrace far more than simply selecting and coaching a football team. He was a showman, with something to sell.

In his weekly column in the *Sunday Express* (and, oddly enough, Gordon Selfridge also had a weekly column – in *The Times!*) Chapman would sometimes feel constrained to apologise for 'preaching commercialism'. However: 'That is the side of football which has become highly important from a managerial point of view.' At Arsenal, he wrote, the question of salesmanship was crucial:

We may not like it but football from the point of view of management is largely a business on a very considerable scale and the clubs may be compared to the big stores and the small shops on the opposite side of the street. One side dresses its windows most attractively to invite trade and the other, less ambitious and venturesome, is content to jog along in much more modest way.

Star players were part of the business calculation. They were important with regard to ambition and pride on the football pitch, but there were, as Chapman wrote, more practical business reasons too:

> The club has a ground of high value either of its own or leased. Thousands of pounds have been spent on it erecting stands, making terraces, and providing all the comforts for spectators that are possible. That is sound business, the commercialism of the showman, if you like . . . Football today is a world's entertainment and it is my responsibility as the showman, . . . to put on the best possible programme.

Thus, football was the 'product' and the players 'the equipment' where Chapman was concerned, and all the celebrated 'innovations' he came up with were designed, first and foremost, to improve the game as a spectacle for the spectators: numbering shirts, floodlights for evening matches, a 45-minute clock for fans to check the length of the game left, clearer and extended markings on the pitch, goal-judges, more open relegation and promotion. Needless to say, they were all rejected by the League and the FA!

But he could alter his own team's shirts and make them more attractive; he could encourage his players to save their money by devising a special saving scheme; and he could promote the club and the players by means of the latest technology: radio and television. Arsenal was the first club to have a match broadcast over radio, and it was the first to take part in experimental televised transmissions.

Selfridge, as would be expected, was first to exploit the publicity possibilities of radio and television – he even had John Logie Baird in the Selfridge basement demonstrating his new invention! But there was one area where Chapman scored a notable victory over his more prestigious counterpart.

Both men were acutely aware of the importance of transport to bring the customers in. When Selfridge had established his store in 1909 he wanted to run a tunnel beneath Oxford Street to Bond Street tube station, and then to rename Bond Street station Selfridges. The Underground company rejected the idea. Chapman, as all the world knows, succeeded in persuading the Underground authorities some

20 years later to change the name of the tube station close to Highbury, from Gillespie Road to Arsenal.

The two men Alec James found himself working for in the autumn of 1929 can without exaggeration, both be considered as visionaries, engaged as they were in extending the known boundaries of their respective worlds. They brought new attitudes to work with them and forced their employees to adopt those attitudes, to look at what they did and how they did it from different angles: 'You have to seek perfection consciously,' Selfridge declared, 'if you don't, you will go on repeating yourself.' And one achieved perfection, he thought, through self-disgust, self-dissatisfaction. Chapman, too, was never satisfied: 'There is one golden rule – no matter how good the team may be, there should always be an attempt to improve it.'

Both men were forever demanding, cajoling, prodding those beneath them and alongside them to come up with new ideas, original thoughts: never should their successful enterprises be allowed to free-wheel for a moment.

Chapman's famous team talks were instituted with this communal spirit-building in mind, rather than for the development of cunning plans and strategies: 'Today men have to make their contribution to a system. Individuality has had to be subordinated to teamwork.'

He had started the pre-match chats at Leeds during the First World War:

I preside at these meetings and, although in the frank discussions a player may feel a little hurt in being singled out for some fault in the previous week's game, a little tact and good humour quickly removed this ... Every man should be encouraged to talk and express his views.

It was usually the more 'individualistic' players who cast doubts upon such gatherings. David Jack recalled James's response to team talks when he first arrived in 1929: 'Though no doubt he found them very interesting, he shared my lack of faith in them. We could not see plans being carried out on the field and we were sceptical as to their value'. The open criticism, he recalled, sometimes got a little hot, but he conceded: 'These talks resulted in at least one very important thing. Many of the Arsenal players were able to make a greater success of their football than would have been the case had they never attended a tactical team meeting.'

James, too, eventually saw their purpose: 'Don't run away with the idea that we won the games by planning out the tactics beforehand.' It was, he thought, the self-criticism that was the main purpose: 'Criticism had to be helpful. If not, it wasn't wanted.'

The team talks had much to do with what Chapman saw as the men's commitment to the club; he attributed much of the success of the team, 'to the fact that our men have had the good sense to realise that their own destiny, as well as that of the club, rested with themselves.'

Arsenal's destiny was much more closely tied to James's own than was Selfridge's, but he could not help but be affected by the glamour of Oxford Street: by the demands of his new job and by the temptations of the glittering world in which it was set.

His immediate boss and the man who signed him on was A. H. Williams, then a director of the store, but originally advertising manager and very much an expert at publicity. Selfridge had told Williams: 'We must give them (the customers) compelling reasons to come to the store – attractions that have nothing to do with shopping but which they feel they must not miss. That's your job, Williams.'

One of the methods adopted had been to have celebrities in the store, people in the news, either as demonstrators or simply as 'exhibits', for autographs. The first Selfridge publicity coup had been in 1909 when they had secured Blériot and his plane. Since then, filmstars, music-hall celebrities, flyers, climbers, famous sportsmen – even inventors – had graced the various departments and windows.

In 1930, Amy Johnson, the sensational female flyer capturing all the headlines, was at Selfridges to open the new aviation department. Later, Suzanne Lenglen would demonstrate tennis on the roof garden. James was, therefore, the latest in a long and celebrated line of the world's top sportsmen and women who had all been used to draw the crowds in. These included Walter Hagen, the golfer, Jack Hobbs, the cricketer and boxing's world heavyweight champion Primo Carnera.

James's arrival was widely publicised and there were pictures of him signing his contract, surrounded by curious on-lookers. He was described as the 'greatest footballer living' and a special window display was devoted entirely to Alex James footballs: he would sign each one bought for the lucky boy or girl, and 'his services and advice will be at the disposal of the customers'.

When one considers that the majority of professional footballers were perfectly happy to disappear from view once the match was over, to their homes, the golf-course, the bowling green, in order to avoid the limelight, James's continual exposure (particularly during that first uncomfortable year at Arsenal when he was the subject of so much vilification and abuse) must have been, initially at least, extremely wearying. Public relations were, after all, in their infancy where sports people were concerned.

At first, as he confessed, he wondered whether or not to resign, but he did start to learn a thing or two about publicity and gradually he grew to like his afternoon trips into the West End:

> Mr A. H. Williams . . . was my boss and he started pointing out to me the value of publicity even to a footballer. He showed me how headlines, pictures and cartoons would put me on the map quite as much as my football skills.
>
> My long shorts were already known. Folks would say, 'That's Alec James, the little fellow in the long knickers.' Publicity for a footballer! But it worked. The store plastered my face and name all over the newspapers and people came into the shop in their hundreds to see the £9,000 new man of Arsenal. I was being built up into something more than just a footballer. I was becoming a crowd-puller already.

However, James would admit in 1937 that the adulation had had its drawbacks:

> My job kept me in the West End in the evenings and I found too many people anxious to show me London by night when I had finished at the store. I fell into parties and found myself at all kinds of queer 'dives' and nightclubs at an hour when any footballer ought to be fast asleep in his bed.
>
> The lights and the flash company went to my head a bit in those early days, or rather nights.

It is difficult to appreciate today just how glamorous a place

Selfridges was in the early Thirties, how different it was from
almost every other store, due mainly to the society life-style and
tastes of Gordon Selfridge himself. The contrast with James's
normal environment of a football stadium was dramatic.

Gordon Selfridge admitted that the appeal of his store was
principally directed at women. It was a period when the rather
severe close-cropped 'boyish' look of the Twenties was softening;
when more women had started wearing make-up, hairstyles were
softer, and clothes had begun to look more and more feminine. And
Selfridge's 'revolution' in retailing consisted, to a large extent, in
stirring the imagination of women by offering them a new world,
by appealing to their sense of beauty. From its sumptuous hanging
gardens on the roof, all the way down to the bargain basement,
women were the target: middle-class women in particular.

'I want them,' Selfridge said, 'to enjoy the warmth, light, colours
and styles and feel fine fabrics.' He once told Williams: 'I helped
emancipate women; I came along just at the time when they wanted
to step out on their own. They came to my store and realised some
of their dreams.'

And so Selfridges was a female environment, a 'social centre', a
place of style and excitement. Even the women employed there
were glamorous: beautiful debutantes from high society often acted
as mannequins at special fashion parades; the famous lift-girls in
their American-style uniforms were regularly being snapped up by
millionaires and married. Every mother, it was said, wanted her
daughter to work at Selfridges.

Alex James, although he protested that he was an innocent at
large ('after all, I was just a Scots lad from very quiet surroundings
and all this London glamour was something I had only read about
till then . . .') had always been a gregarious, sociable chap; from
Kirkcaldy on, he had never been one to shirk the opportunity to
befriend members of the opposite sex. He was also a man very much
aware of his appearance, indeed, unlikely as it may sound, there
was something of the dandy about him.

Clothes were a source of pleasure and pride to him and only the
best would do. He had developed luxurious tastes such as silk shirts
and pyjamas; he wore the best-cut suits and went to his own tailor
to have them made. Not even Selfridges' best were good enough
for him – indeed he was not at all loyal to his employer's products

– except for a regular flow of the latest-style Aertex shirts he supplied to the Arsenal dressing-room.

His tastes became more sophisticated when he settled in London: no more loud, garish tartan checks, though he was still flamboyant and very much 'in style.' He was also very fastidious about the details of his appearance: nails and hands, for instance. He regularly went to a manicurist (much to Peggy's surprise, who only found out when the shop rang up concerning a missed appointment). He went to a hairdresser in Piccadilly; he even turned up at home one morning with red toe-nails! The story was that he had been visited by a Chinese chiropractor 'at a friend's house' and had fallen asleep, only to wake up with his toe-nails painted. It was close to the end of the season and, when the James family teamed up with David Jack and his family on holiday in Devon, he had to keep his sandals on to avoid embarrassment. How he came to be sleeping in a friend's house with a Chinaman painting his toe-nails was never fully explained; but, then, there would always remain areas of mystery about his life. As Peggy, his wife, commented:

> Mrs Jack said to me, 'Where do you think Alec goes every evening?' and I said, 'I don't really care as long as he comes home.' If it hadn't been for my tolerance, I suppose the marriage wouldn't have lasted. Whether he had eyes for other women, I wouldn't know. He always used to say to me, 'One's enough for me.'

Girl-friends or not, being part of the glittering, privileged world of Selfridges, mingling with the celebrities, dancing to the top bands in the ballroom, rubbing shoulders with theatre luminaries, watching the fashion shows in the Palm Court, all contributed to the sense of frustration and impatience he felt with his lot as a professional footballer.

For in 1931, the contract with Selfridges ended. James's weekly wage returned to the £8 basic that all professionals received. His bubble burst.

His response was immediate. He refused to sign on for Arsenal unless Chapman offered him more money. Chapman, of course, could do no such thing and so James, rather noisily, declared himself a free agent.

During his summer-long 'strike' there was speculation in the press as to what he was up to. Some claimed that he was making a selfless protest against the maximum wage. In the very same year the Players Union was making approaches to the FA and the League, pointing out the 'paltry' rewards for successful players reaching the Cup Final. Though transfer fees were reaching £10,000 and receipts at Wembley were topping £25,000, a player received £8 for playing in the final, £4 for appearing in a semi-final and only £1 for a drawn game.

In the *Daily Sketch,* James refuted such 'idealistic' ideas:

> I haven't the slightest intention of posing either as a martyr or as a crusader fighting to right the wrongs of the oppressed brothers of my profession. In football – off the field, I mean, of course, – it must always be each man for himself. And professional footballers didn't invent that rule.

There was only one man who could look after Alex James – and that was Alex James.

By not signing, of course, he avoided the Arsenal summer tour: 'I objected to the idea of a tour at the end of the sort of strenuous season I had had. There was no money in that tour for me and, as a pleasure trip – well, I just didn't want it.'

So, instead of joining in the fun and games in Denmark and Sweden, he motored up to Carnoustie for the Open Golf Championships with Phil Kelso, an old friend. Being unsigned, of course, he was free to consider many offers that soon came pouring in of alternative employment but, unfortunately, most of the offers were just stunts. Inevitably, America featured: one promoter offered him £1,000 and a percentage of the gate receipts for a series of exhibitions. But America was too much of a gamble. There would also be the problem of re-entering British football once the trip was over and, for this reason, an offer from Spain for £1,000 and £20 a match was also turned down. There was a 'vaudeville' proposal of £15 a week, and an offer of a public house in Ireland in exchange for a season with Drumcondra (ironically, the Irish club would get their man almost a decade later when James played in a couple of friendly matches for them at the beginning of the Second World War). Someone wrote to offer James the proprietorship of a

It's an Old Spanish Custom   By TOM WEBSTER

HEARING THAT
SPANISH
FOOTBALLERS GET
AS MUCH AS
£30 A WEEK
ALEC
JAMES ARRIVES
AT THE ARSENAL
OFFICES
PREPARED TO
DISCUSS NEW
TERMS.

The above cartoon appeared in a greater part of our editions yesterday

nightclub in Rhyl, but just how seriously James took any of these proposals is hard to say.

He later claimed that he had been expecting Herbert Chapman to give in: 'Quite honestly, I thought Herbert Chapman would come to heel under my "strike" when I refused to sign for Arsenal that season, but it seemed that I didn't know my man.' But he must have known that Chapman could make no offers that went beyond the maximum wage. However, the idea that Chapman simply remained aloof from everything and let James sweat it out was refuted by James as, close to the beginning of the 1931/32 season, he prepared to return:

> Statements have appeared from time to time that the Arsenal manager, Mr Herbert Chapman, has not seen or heard from me since the last playing season. Actually, he has twice been to see me during the summer – the last time was at my house only a week or so ago. He failed to persuade me to sign on because the plans concerning my career apart from football had not then completely matured. My business affairs have now been adjusted to my entire satisfaction and I am ready to start football – if wanted.

James eventually began training, first at Bournemouth's ground, and later at Nottingham with father-in-law Dave Willis. And two weeks before the season was to begin, it was announced that he had signed on. Beneath a headline: 'Mr Chapman Gets A Shock', it was reported that a *Sunday Express* reporter had rung Mr Chapman and asked him if he knew that Alex James had signed on.

> 'What!!' roared Mr Chapman.
> 'Yes, it's quite true,' said the voice. 'Alex signed on at 11 o'clock this morning.'
> 'What!!' bellowed Mr Chapman again. 'Who for?'
> 'Selfridges,' said the voice in a whisper.

Had it all been a long-running publicity stunt, cooked up by James and Selfridges director A. H. Williams? If so, it had been an elaborate one. James denied the accusation, claiming that he was as surprised as anyone with the new Selfridges offer, especially as it involved a rise to £300. He also won another 'ghosted' newspaper column, this time with the more lively *Sunday Graphic and Sunday*

News. The *Graphic's* sister paper, the *Daily Sketch,* announced on Saturday that he would be going along to Highbury the following Monday to sign on: crowds gathered to watch him go in. Chapman, predictably, was not there to greet him, though some of the players are said to have raided the band-room to give him an impromptu mock-musical fanfare. It must have been like greeting the return of a celebrated truant back to boarding school.

What Chapman made of it all is hard to say. Publicity, after all, was not something he shied away from, but this had been different: the endless press speculation, the pictures of James on the beach with his arms around the bathing belles, the cartoons and the jokey features had hardly contributed to the sense of dignity Chapman liked to foster where the club was concerned. And yet, he probably conceded that it was the price one paid for success. Times were changing and no one knew that better than Chapman: 'The life we lead is so different; the pace, the excitement, and the sensationalism which we crave are new factors which have had a disturbing influence. They have upset the old balance mentally as well as physically . . .

15

Tactical Triumph

There were few thrills in football to match that of an Arsenal breakaway goal. The ball would be cleared from the defence, then a long pass in front of Hulme, a fast burst of 30 yards and an accurate centre volleyed first time by Lambert. There would be perhaps 10 seconds from one goal-mouth to the other.   Bernard Joy, *Forward Arsenal*

Arsenal's methods are their own and should remain their own because they have special men to play this special game.
'Scrutator' in the *Glasgow Evening Times,* September 1930

THE SEASON THAT followed the FA Cup win saw Arsenal secure the league championship with a team that must be considered one of the classical football elevens of all time.

The only significant alterations from the Cup Final team were Roberts for Seddon at centre-half; Keyser and Harper to share the goalkeeper's position with Preedy; Jones for Baker at right-half. It was still not a team of outstanding individuals but it was a team that had a system, a style and a collective personality that proved devastating to opponents.

They lost only four games all season and won 25. They scored 127 goals, one short of the Aston Villa record of 128, a total that helped Villa into second place that season. Sheffield Wednesday, confidently expected to complete a hat trick of championship wins, were left trailing in third place, some 14 points adrift!

But Arsenal did more than just win a title: they captured the football public's imagination and became the most talked about team in the League's long history. Crowds flocked to see them, to watch the 'machine' that could outwit opponents week in and week out, sometimes infuriatingly by sleight of hand, almost; at others in devastating, breath-taking fashion. Arsenal's game was the 'modern' game that Chapman had said the public demanded. It was in

THE CLASSICS.

By TOM WEBSTER.

THE BEST EVER.
(IN MY RECOLLECTION.)

No 1. ALEC JAMES.
THE CLEVEREST FOOTBALLER THAT HAS BEEN SEEN FOR 20 YEARS.

NO GENTLEMAN IN MY TIME HAS EVER SHOWN SUCH FIENDISH FOOT-WORK AS ALEC JAMES THE INSIDE-LEFT OF THE ARSENAL AND SCOTLAND.

JUST ABOUT 1911 IN A YOUTH FULL OF IDOLATRY I THOUGHT Joe Bache OF ASTON VILLA WAS SUPREME

JOE BACHE WAS EQUALLY GOOD AT INSIDE-LEFT OR OUTSIDE-LEFT AND HE COULD RUN LIKE A TRAIN.

WITH JOSEPH VICTOR BACHE LOSING A FEW YARDS IN HIS ANNIHILATION OF SPACE MY CHOICE OSCILLATED TOWARDS Charles Buchan OF SUNDERLAND

FOLLOWING YEARS OF WAR AND POSSIBLY INDISCRETION I REGARDED William Walker ALSO OF ASTON VILLA AS THE MOST CUNNING

AS A PURE MATCH WINNER PERHAPS I WOULD PREFER Dixie Dean OF EVERTON BUT I STILL THINK THAT

JAMES MUST GO DOWN AS THE CLEVEREST FOOTBALLER I HAVE EVER SEEN.

BUT WHAT HAPPENS TO A CLEVER FOOTBALLER? I WILL TELL YOU. HE IS GENERALLY VICTIMISED BY OPPONENTS WHO CANNOT PLAY.

YOU - DEAR READER SHOULD HAVE SEEN ALEX JACKSON'S LEGS AFTER CHELSEA'S CUP TIE WITH BLACKBURN ROVERS. PAINTED ALL OVER WITH 'ODINE JACKSON ALMOST SAID "I'M NOT JACKSON. I'M BIG CHIEF PALE-FACE OF WALHAM GREEN."

OF COURSE THIS IS FOUL PLAY. BUT WHAT ARE WE GOING TO DO ABOUT IT? THE ANSWER IS THE SAME AS THE REFEREE'S. NOTHING!

TOM WEBSTER 31

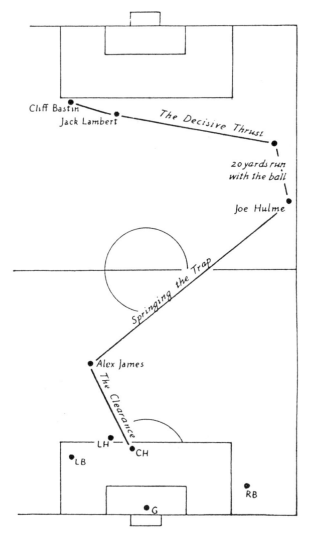

Cliff Bastin

Jack Lambert

The Decisive Thrust

20 yards run
with the ball

Joe Hulme

Springing the Trap

Alex James

The Clearance

LH

• LB

CH

RB

• G

Arsenal's ten-second goal which changed the face of football.

tune with 'the bustle and excitement of every day life' being a 'fast-moving spectacle with, rapier-like attacks that have the spirit of adventure about them'.

No one seemed out of place in the team; all were comfortable in the positions they held and were thus able to realise their talents completely. As Joe Mercer has said, 'tactics are to enable people to express themselves naturally' and there was something about the Arsenal team at this time that was almost a force of nature.

Full backs Tom Parker and Eddie Hapgood combined experience and youth, solid dependability with flair and arrogance. Between them, in the infamous 'stopper' centre-half position, Herbie Roberts was unflappable, powerful, uncomplicated and immune to the bar-rackers on the terraces who thought him crude. He possessed skill enough to keep up a constant supply of passes to the men closest at hand who could release the ball forward, half-backs Bob John and Charlie Jones. Jones was fast and decisive in the tackle, equally at home as a full back when he played for Wales; John was also fast, having once been a winger and a good passer of the ball. These three half-backs were supplemented by Seddon on occasions, solid and dependable as he had been in the 1930 Cup Final.

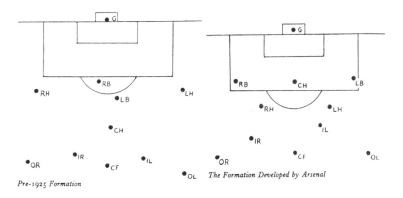

Pre-1925 Formation

The Formation Developed by Arsenal

The system they developed was far ahead of its time in organisation and co-operation: while the centre-half stood close upon the heels of the opposing centre-forward, the full backs often gave space to opposing wingers, held back from tackling while manoevring and retreating as the rest of the defence took up position in the goal-mouth. The full backs and centre-half worked a complicated covering system, helped by the half-backs, the whole scheme designed to lure the opposition further and deeper in order that the eventual breakout would catch as many opponents stranded up field and out of position as possible.

Up front, Joe Hulme was one of the fastest wingers in Britain, an accurate crosser of the ball and a goalscorer; Cliff Bastin on the left was equally swift, cool and intelligent, now covering both left-side positions; Jack Lambert at centre-forward was more rough and ready in style but a prolific goalscorer with both feet and head; David Jack, at inside right, (who 'slides past you like a pane of glass sliding by') was an inside forward from an earlier era, but was equally at home in this one, switching position according to the point of attack, and another player adept at finishing.

The bulk of the scoring was done by these four men, indeed, amazing as it may seem today for a team that scored 127 goals in a season, the four forwards mentioned scored 111 of them (five more coming from James and seven from stand-in forwards). The half-backs and full backs contributed a mere four goals – and between 1930 and 1937, of 683 goals scored in the League by Arsenal, just 28 were scored by non-forwards. Thus, the 'flexibility' of Arsenal's play was a long way from post-war 'total' football, where half-backs and full backs are expected to contribute their share of goals. However, as Bernard Joy has said:

> Arsenal changed the functions of every position vitally, except that of the goalkeeper, and even he had to adjust his movements to the new alignment of the backs. It was almost as though Herbert Chapman had put the players in a box, shaken them thoroughly and scattered them over the field again.

Of all the changes, though, the most 'revolutionary' was that which involved Alex James: free to roam wherever he liked, performing a role rather than holding a position, he was the first truly 'modern' player.

For opposing right-halves looking across for him to mark it must have been a puzzling experience. Joe Mercer recalled:

> James was always too deep in his own half to be tackled – and he often hardly held the ball at all – so you were floundering about

wondering what to do. As for marking him out of the game by
'shadowing' him, you may lay your plans for subduing him and
watch these plans to complete success for an hour. James may
appear to be wandering about in a state of mental hopelessness.
Suddenly he is unmarked, picks up a stray ball and with a sway,
a stagger and a pass he has opened up an easy path for a goal.

James had, as Frank Curruthers put it in 1932: 'entered his Kingdom and wherever he plays he is acclaimed not simply for his show-
manship and his tricks and subterfuges but for his magical football
craft. He has no equal'.

To liken him and what he did to other great 'schemers' such as
Jimmy Seed and Clem Stevenson was only to say that, like them,
he created opportunities, made goals, was a general rather than a
foot soldier. But there was no way to describe just *how* he did all
this in training manual terms. David Jack conceded as much in his
book *Soccer,* written in 1934: 'James has to be dealt with at some
length because he is a definite contradiction to many of the qualities
I shall eventually stress as being essential to the development of the
successful player in the position.'

Jack went on to say that James lacked marksmanship, heading
ability and speed.

Thus it must be clearly understood that he cannot be accepted as
a model for young players, because his defects would be an in-
surmountable handicap to the ordinary footballer. James is not
an ordinary footballer; he is an outstanding example of the
'natural' school.

Jack's comments concerning James's natural abilities could, if
taken out of context, have given the impression that James had not
had to work hard to become the player he was. James himself did
not help matters in his ghosted column for the London *Evening Star*
in 1930, telling budding young players to 'be in the right place at
the right time' and to 'try and think two, even three moves ahead'.
Similarly unhelpful was his comment that the secret of the Arsenal
system was to find a player like himself: 'Nearly every team has
such a player in the ranks; if not, they should move heaven and earth
to get one'!

James certainly did possess a natural talent but he had been

strong-willed and dedicated enough to follow his instincts and develop his game beyond the confines of the traditional positions as they were then understood. In every team he had played for, from Ashfield right through to Arsenal, he had 'wandered', had sought to draw the game around him, and he had been harshly criticised for doing so.

At Arsenal, he had discovered a perfect set-up (even though the period of adjustment had almost ended in disaster). It was a mistake to talk, as Jack did, of James having 'sacrificed' his goal-scoring habit, or to say that he had cut out 'frills and fancy work in order to fit into the team'. James was first and foremost, a team player: team in the psychological sense of men thinking together, reading one another's minds, as it were, being at one. Thus, to score a goal was the job of the team. James had scored goals at Preston because there had been no one else to do it (rather in the same way that an American Football quarterback sometimes runs with the ball when all the receivers are covered). At Arsenal, he did not need to go forward – there were plenty of others well able to finish off the moves that he began.

His dribbling skills, too, he saw as being purely functional: not an aesthetic extra, something he did for the fun of it. He never taunted men with his skills; as an opponent once said:

> He tricked you, but not to make a fool of you. Some players annoyed you by the superior air they adopted when dribbling. Alex never does that; he just wheels round and round and you follow him blindly and dummy-like, believing that he might fall down and thus give you a chance to get the ball.

This deadly earnest approach to what, for spectators, was great fun, only added to the amusement:

> His footwork is entrancing and amazingly deft. Many times he drives the spectators into gales of laughter by the tricks he plays on opponents and the nonchalant way in which he performs them. And, as amusing as anything, is that this sturdy little fellow . . . never smiles himself. Nothing he does is amusing to himself . . . whether he leaves an opponent wondering how he has been beaten or whether he himself is rolled in the mud, James shows the same worried little frown in his chubby face until Arsenal supporters can scarcely look at him without laughing.
> *Sunday Dispatch,* February 1931

It is often claimed that he enjoyed his football at Preston and Raith more than at Arsenal, where everything was grind and mechanics. Times were certainly more carefree for him before he came to Arsenal: there was less responsibility, more opportunity for youthful excess. Something (ostensibly, pursuit of money) had always driven James on to greater things, but until he came to Highbury he had too often been dismissed as a 'luxury' player, an 'individualist' and a mere 'trickster'. Now he was the kingpin of one of the greatest teams of the decade and his behaviour, his whole demeanour, proved how much of a team man he was.

Chapman was certainly in no doubt as to his commitment, as is shown in his description of an incident in 1933 when James had been badly injured in a match against Birmingham. He had been carried off, and Chapman had wanted him to go straight to hospital but James insisted on staying on in the dressing-room, though in pain. Chapman wrote:

> When the players came off the field at half-time he was lying on the table still suffering acutely but it was evident that his thoughts were still on the match and he called to me and suggested the adoption of tactics which he believed might make up for his absence from the field and possibly lead to the scoring of one or more goals. The players went out and shortly afterwards he heard the muffled sound of cheering and he insisted on knowing what had happened. When he was told that Jack had scored he raised his head from the table and clapped his hands, telling how deep was his interest in the Arsenal team even in so much pain.

As the seasons rolled by, opposing teams proved unable to halt Arsenal's progress. Following the 1931 championship win, Arsenal almost won the Double in 1932 – runners-up in the League and beaten Cup Finalists. For the next three years of 1933, 1934 and 1935 they were champions. In 1936 they won the Cup again and in 1938 they were League champions once more. Such sustained mastery of powerful League opponents achieved in the context of what was unquestionably the world's toughest League tournament had not been witnessed before, nor would it be again until Liverpool's 'machine' began rolling in the 1960s.

Comparisons are misleading but significant similarities can be noted, in particular the influence of a group of 'back-room' men who were able to continue the lessons from decade to decade, all having played a part in forming the original plan. The disruption of new men coming in from outside the 'family' was avoided. Tom Whittaker, Joe Shaw, John Peters, Bob Wall were as much a team as the men on the park, and all were imbued with Chapman's methods, philosophy and ideals. Add to that, Chapman's preference for intelligent, thoughtful players such as Parker, Jack, Crayston and James and one can see how Liverpool's 'boot-room' is hardly unique.

With such background continuity, the replacement of players

who either retired or were injured was achieved in an almost seamless way: the faces changed but the machine rolled on, smoothly, sometimes even more efficiently.

Thus, centre-forward Jack Lambert was replaced by Ted Drake; Tom Parker by George Male; Bob John and Charlie Jones by Crayston and Copping; David Jack by Reg Bowden, Bobby Davidson and Eddie Coleman; Joe Hulme by Alf Kirchen and Pat Beasley. And, right across that incredible decade, a set of players endured. Bob John, Cliff Bastin, Eddie Hapgood, Herbie Roberts – all these men were at Highbury when James arrived in 1929 and would continue after he had retired in 1937.

Where Arsenal and Liverpool diverge most dramatically, however, is over the question of tactics and here, sadly, history has been unkind to Arsenal.

The historian C. L. Mowat, talking of the National Government that came to power in 1931, said:

> From its triumph in 1931 it shambled its unimaginative way to its fall in 1940 . . . . Its responses were not bold, it retreated before aggression; it rearmed but at first too slowly . . . in retrospect, it has been blamed for all the misfortunes of the time, partly because its opponents rose to power by reiterating their version of its history and its period.

And in football terms, Arsenal's reputation has suffered a similar fate; critics have attached a 'safety-first' tag to it similar to that attached to the National Government of the day. Arsenal F.C., triumphant and innovative in 1931, came to be blamed for the increasingly mechanical, stereotyped and unadventurous football played in Great Britain by the majority of clubs, and eventually by the national teams.

> Arguments are going round as to how long Arsenal can keep their present 'negative' style of football and continue to draw big crowds. The world loves a lover – and a winner – but the safety-first football of the Gunners seems to be losing some of its appeal. One harmful result of the club's peculiar style is that other clubs have copied it. And not having the players to do it, much drab football has been our weekly portion.
>   'The Major' in *Thomson's Weekly News*, 1935

If blame is to be apportioned for the 'decline' in English football standards when measured against the progress occurring on the Continent, then it must lie elsewhere. The Arsenal of the 1930s was constructed first and foremost as a response to the demands of English League football.

Chapman was well aware of the accusations levelled at his team:

> Unfortunately, we aren't allowed to study style. So severe is the competition that we are compelled to sacrifice whatever ambitions we may have for effect. With us, it is a case of goals and points. At times one is persuaded that nothing else matters.

However, he knew that his team strategy was complex, clearly

Note the sandals, as James reports at Highbury on the last day of July, 1934, to begin training — shown below with Male, Copping and Moss on the left, James in the foreground — for the coming season. (BBC Hulton Picture Library)

A rare action shot of Alex James —here he leaves behind the other baffled players, including Matt Busby (third from right) in a match against Manchester City on 13 October 1934.

On 25 April 1936, Arsenal—captained by James—won the F A Cup Final 1-0 against Sheffield United, which led to celebrations at the Café Royal. The ladies in the picture are Mrs James and Mrs Male, the players Jack Crayston, Alex James, Ted Drake, George Male, Cliff Bastin and Alf Kirchen.

thought out and needed study to be understood properly – a study
he was sure would take a long time, given the traditional English
abhorrence of 'coaching' and 'science'. 'We English are slow. It
will do for years.' And he was right, of course, though he added that
he would come up with something new when everyone had finally
adopted Arsenal's style. Unfortunately, Chapman died in 1934 and
so Arsenal continued in the direction he had set. Chapman's
replacement, George Allison; was a journalist and broadcaster, not
a football tactician. He bought Ted Drake, and Drake's goals won
Arsenal the League in 1935. Meanwhile, Whittaker and Shaw
continued to refine the Arsenal defensive system and the success
simply continued.

Arsenal would always frustrate and bamboozle League clubs
who refused to use imagination to overcome them, who looked
instead for a Dixie Dean to batter the walls down – long hopeful
balls lofted on to soaring heads. Even Everton, that citadel of football excellence, finally conceded. Early in the decade, their director
Cuff had admonished players for trying out the dreaded Arsenal
Third Back system. But in 1938, according to Joe Mercer, they did
adopt Arsenal's style – and they won the League. Until that time,
Mercer said, the general response of many players, particularly in
the north, had been to sneer at Arsenal: 'The buggers can't play!' It
was an attitude shared by many millions of spectators north of
Watford who also failed to understand the Arsenal style, 'Lucky
Arsenal' being the popular response from the terraces.

In a sense, though, this refusal to acknowledge Arsenal's skills
reflected a resentment felt north of London towards the increasingly prosperous south. Arsenal, in their bright expensive-looking new
red shirts, stepping from their private railway carriage, parading
their expensive stars: good-looking Hapgood, debonair Crayston,
aristocratic Jack and jazzy little James were the perfect target.

George Scott in *Up The Boro: Middlesbrough in the 30's,* gave a
chilling picture of such emotions: as a young boy he was taken to
Ayresome Park, and he saw how cruel the crowd could be towards
visiting footballers with boos and jeers escalating to more virulent
abuse, contemptuous nicknames 'apparently inane but deeply
poisonous when shouted by several thousand voices of hate.'
However,

The enmity of the Middlesbrough crowd was given complete

unity and its greatest power when the visitors to Ayresome Park were Arsenal. This team of remarkable talents represented wealth and privilege. They came from the soft south, from London, from the city of government where, it was imagined, all social evil was plotted and directed against places like Teesside. The Arsenal club could afford to pay large sums in transfer fees to buy the best players. The players themselves enjoyed comforts and amenities such as no other club could afford to provide. They carried themselves with pride and played with a stylistic beauty. They were fine footballers and had a long history of victory.

All these things combined to inflame the hatred of the Middlesbrough crowd, and once I saw hundreds of men climb over the barriers and thrust past the police and pour on to the field, intending to do injury to the Arsenal team. This was the final explosion of hatred which more often restricted itself to words or at most the throwing of orange peel, cigarette packets or an occasional bottle. I still remember the spectacle with feelings of fear and horror.

As George Male recalled years later, 'we were hated all right. They came in their thousands to watch us get hammered – that was all the enjoyment they got out of it'.

Easy to understand, therefore, the almost nationwide frenzy of excitement and glee that greeted Arsenal's shock defeat in the Cup by Walsall in 1933. This was more than just a giant-killing act (though it will serve as the model for all time); this was the slaying of the Dragon. The fact that it had been achieved by good old 'get-stuck-in' methods only made it the more laudable in the eyes of those, like Brown's Middlesbrough supporters, who had an irrational hatred for, a gut envy of, what was perceived as 'privilege'.

It was all extremely good box-office, of course; crowds flocked to watch the Gunners in the hope that their guns would be well and truly spiked. Yet it was certainly the case that the crowds would not have flocked so eagerly and in such vast numbers, particularly to Highbury, had Alex James not been wearing an Arsenal shirt.

No player in my lifetime has had the drawing power of 'Wee Alec'. I can best emphasise the statement by telling you that when it was announced that James was unfit and a doubtful starter, the Arsenal telephones never ceased ringing on the preceding Friday and Saturday morning. From places as far afield as Eastbourne, Brighton and Bognor, yes, even from Swindon and Northampton and other distant spots came the anxious query: 'Is James playing today?' George Allison in the *Daily Express*, 8 June 1953

Chapman understood the importance of James from an entertainment point of view; there is an apocryphal story that he ordered James to cut out the circus tricks until the team was 3-0 up, but it was clear that James was a man apart, worth his weight in gold at the turnstiles, win or lose. In that sense, Chapman, in securing James and building his team around him, was able to have it both ways: success, built on a 'negative' system of defence, yet glorious, unforgettable, entertaining...

They have so much confidence in themselves that they are content to play an apparently defensive game. They let their opponents bring the ball up and appear to be defending desperately. Then, in a twinkling, James picks up the ball from the ruck and the Arsenal forwards are away through a scattered defence. Alex Jackson in the *Glasgow Evening Times*, April 1931

AN UNRECORDED TRICKY BIT OF CONJURING BY ALEC JAMES THE ARSENAL WIZARD AT THE FOOTBALLERS' XMAS PARTY

16

The War of Words

Chapman and I, both obstinate and super-confident in our own ability, battled all the time. We were always having verbal warfare.

Alex James in the *News of the World,* 1937

THE ACCEPTED IMAGE of Herbert Chapman bequeathed to us by a clutch of Arsenal autobiographies published after the Second World War is that of a much loved but sometimes feared headmaster: kind, caring but stern and occasionally unforgiving. He was much loved because he exhibited a 'common touch', was ready to muck in with the players, to play golf or trot round the pitch occasionally. Feared, not because he had the power to dismiss a man (which he obviously had to do from time to time) but because one of his talents was that of knowing the weaknesses of his players, of knowing how to keep them mentally 'on their toes' by surprising them, catching them with their guard down. George Male's tale of being taken aside briefly in a tunnel beneath a railway line as the team was making its way to the train and being told, out of the blue, that he should 'pull his socks up' because he was 'playing for his place' was typical Chapman psychology: 'He read me like a book. He'd never have told me that in front of the rest of the team: I would have clammed up with embarrassment. But I thought about it from then on and wondered what I should do.'

Whether he was challenging Eddie Hapgood's sense of personal pride, or digging away at David Jack's sense of duty, Chapman was a past master at man-management.

Where Alex James was concerned, the theory was that Chapman shrewdly allowed him more rope than anyone else; that James was able to get away with various indiscretions because he was special and because everyone knew this and thus it set no precedents.

James, however, would not have seen it in quite the same light, and it is clear that there was something about James that Chapman could not fathom. Their verbal warfare often took Chapman to the very brink of his patience and beyond:

'You have caused me more sleepless nights than any man I have ever known!' James claimed Chapman told him once.

'Well, you're not exactly a nightcap to me, either!' was the James response.

There was not to be a season that did not include some celebrated row, some difference of opinion: from 1931 onwards when James enlivened the close season by refusing to sign on, right up until the end of 1933, a couple of months before Chapman's death, the battles raged.

What upset Chapman most was that James enjoyed having arguments in public; that he would use the press to challenge Chapman's authority, try to force the great man out into the open. He failed in 1931; Chapman had sat tight and James had been able to return to the fold with his pride intact. In 1932, however, he dragged Chapman into a public row just before the Cup Final – a row that had unfortunate consequences for just about everyone.

Arsenal had reached the Final during a successful couple of months that had seen them win 14 out of 15 Cup and League matches. By 26 March, they were heading for the Double – a feat not achieved since Preston's Invincibles.

However, against West Ham on that Saturday, James was carried off the field with a bad knee injury. In the following League matches, played without him, Arsenal's form slumped: the team won just one game out of five and on Cup Final day, Everton, six points in the lead, was destined to take the League Championship.

James still had hopes of playing in the Cup Final against Newcastle; he and Joe Hulme, also injured, were left in London while the team travelled to Brighton for a week of special training – but as Tom Whittaker recalled:

Both were considered unfit by Mr Chapman and so unavailable for Wembley. I was not so sure that they were completely unfit, but Chapman was the boss and he had made the decision. Then things began to happen. On Wednesday 20 April, three days before the Final, the Daily Mail carried under the signature of

The Red Hope   By TOM WEBSTER

FOR ALL THOSE HOT GLOWING FIERY AND FERVID SUPPORTERS OF THE ARSENAL

HERE IS SOME GOOD NEWS.

ALEC JAMES IS PRACTICALLY CERTAIN TO PLAY IN THE CUP FINAL.

WHEN HE HEARD THE GLAD TIDINGS AN ARSENAL SPECTATOR WHO HAS SUPPORTED THE TEAM THROUGH THICK AND THIN EVER SINCE LAST WEDNESDAY

BREATHED FOUR DIFFERENT SIZES OF RELIEF AND —— STARTED TO RUN IN HIS SLEEP.

FOR THE BENEFIT OF THE UNINITIATED ALEC JAMES HAD —— A BAD KNEE

BUT UNDER THE EXHORTATIONS LAMENTATIONS AND HOT FOMENTATIONS OF THE ARSENAL TRAINER THE KNEE HAS LISTENED TO REASON.

GAZING ON THE KNEE MORE IN HOPE THAN EXPECTATION, HE SAID

THAT THE ARSENAL SUPPORTERS NEED NOT WORRY AS HE THINKS ALEC JAMES COULD PLAY BETTER WITH ONE LEG THAN MOST PLAYERS COULD WITH TWO.

'Arbiter', Mr Frank Carruthers, the exclusive news of the team for Wembley. This was the eleven given to him by Mr Chapman: Moss, Parker, Hapgood, Jones, Roberts, Male, Beasley, Jack, Lambert, Bastin, John. Note the absence of Hulme and James, and the inclusion of Pat Beasley at outside right.
In London the two men who had been left out read the story.

James had been under the impression that, had he been fit, he would have played.

Then, to our dismay, we saw in the evening papers that the Arsenal team had been chosen and neither Joe nor I was in it.
By this time we both considered ourselves fit so I said to Joe: 'I'm not standing for this. I'm going to ring up Fleet Street, tell them we're fit and get them to ask why we have not been chosen.'

The man contacted was L. V. Manning of the *Daily Sketch* – a colleague of James's on the sister paper of the *Sunday Graphic*. Manning had the two men photographed at Highbury running round the pitch and the next morning the *Sketch* carried the picture and the story headlined: 'The Two Fittest Men In Football Are Out Of The Cup Final!'

When he read the paper at our Brighton hotel, Mr Chapman was furious. He telephoned Highbury, threatened to sack old John Peters, the Assistant Secretary, for allowing Manning and the photographer on to the pitch, and ordered James and Hulme to be sent down to Brighton on the first possible train.

Chapman, his authority having been questioned at such a crucial moment, was still the publicist, according to Whittaker, and thus he tried to turn this bizarre situation to his advantage. News was leaked that there would be a 'secret' fitness trial the following morning. A horde of photographers was thus on hand when Joe Hulme was put through a series of workouts and was passed fit. Poor Pat Beasley, in the Cup Final team on Wednesday, was now out on Friday.
Next came James, and another tough workout: 'We blocked and tackled him; made him chase the ball; cross it with either foot; swerve, sprint.' James, too, passed the test. He was back in the Cup Final team.

At this point, however, accounts differ. According to Whittaker, a late photographer called out for one last shot. James returned, obligingly, and went into a tackle with Whittaker – and collapsed. His knee had 'gone' again.

According to James, however, it was Chapman who had called him back when he had already changed back into his 'civvy'clothes.

> I changed back into playing togs and went out. The manager told me to go into a tackle with Tom Whittaker. I did – and my knee went again. I limped back to the dressing-room, all hopes of Wembley gone. I was raving mad about it and Herbert Chapman was almost crying.

Whittaker's account takes up the story: 'We carried him into the dressing-room . . . Alec, almost crying in pain and disappointment, wouldn't let the doctor touch him and shouted at me to get everybody out of the dressing-room. Even Chapman had to go.'

As James rather harshly put it later: 'Chapman was a great showman . . . and it was that trait in his make-up which robbed me of a Cup Final medal.'

Arsenal went on to lose the Final. Chapman's second reshuffle of the team (promoting half-back John to inside left and introducing George Male at left half for his first ever Cup tie) proved, in retrospect, to be a miscalculation which even the ever-loyal Bastin admitted. Both Chapman and James might have admitted letting the other down, James by forcing Chapman's hand by breaking club rules concerning the use of the press and publicity where team matters were concerned; Chapman by allowing James to influence his team selection at a crucial time.

The following season, 1932/33, saw yet another row spill out into the public domain, spoiling what should have been yet another Arsenal triumph: their second championship win in a row.

Once again, it was an argument centring around a point of principle. With the championship won and with one fixture to go, Chapman arranged for the team to travel to Ireland for a friendly match as part of a transfer deal. James did not want to go. Having played 40 matches that season: 'I considered I had done enough to be worth my pay. After all, I was no spring chicken by that time and I took a deuce of a lot of punishment in my matches.'

He did not go; Chapman apparently made no comment. But the following week, with the final fixture of the season at Sheffield approaching, James claims he found himself being kept in the dark about the arrangements for travelling and so on. There was also no word about whether he had been selected. In fact, he was extremely anxious to play in order to create a personal record of 41 League matches in a season. But still no word came from Highbury. 'By this time I gathered there something fishy in the wind, so in my cussed way I took my wife to the pictures and decided to forget all about Sheffield and the match.'

Relations with Chapman thus soured, James felt he could not attend the banquet thrown by the League to celebrate Arsenal's championship win, a function attended by all the top football dignitaries. Needless to say, James came in for much criticism, C. E. Sutcliffe, a League official, feeling that he had insulted just about everybody, and McKenna, President of the League, calling James a 'baby'. James saw it differently:

Here I was, condemned as a temperamental, silly, spoiled football star, when all the time it was only Herbert Chapman's way of hitting back at me for refusing to go to Ireland. Do you wonder that I began to find life at Highbury a little disturbing?

The year of 1933 was indeed a troubled one, and a sad one, when one considers that it was to be Chapman's last as a manager. The defeat at Walsall in January had shaken both him and the club, causing great embarrassment. Chapman felt that a major restructuring of the playing staff was called for; in the League, James's injury continued to plague him and he played only a dozen games before Christmas 1933; in November, after a great deal of criticism of James from people claiming that he was mixing with the 'wrong sort of company', Chapman responded by arranging for James to have a holiday, first in Bournemouth and then on a cargo boat heading for Boulogne! James, expecting something better, still took it all in good part, extorting extra cash from the much put-upon John Peters, assistant to Chapman, who had been assigned the task of seeing James off. The rest, James declared, did him good, but it was unnecessary. All the wild party talk, he explained was nonsense: 'Herbert Chapman believed all those crazy stories and decided that

Tottenham Hotspur Football & Athletic Company, Limited.

Official Programme

And Record of the Club.

Issued every Match Day. **PRICE ONE PENNY.**

VOL. XXVI. No 7. SEPTEMBER 16, 1933.

the only thing to be done was to get me right away for a time.' James returned in November; within a few weeks, Chapman was taken ill and in January he died.

James, along with the rest of the Arsenal 'family', was greatly shocked: 'He [Chapman] was to my mind the only real genius football has ever seen. Picture a middle-aged man, genial and smiling, shirt-sleeves rolled up, jacket off. Bubbling over with dynamic personality. A leader of men.'

And yet, James would always harbour reservations: 'I did not like the way Chapman did certain things: he didn't like my way either. So we bickered on, neither giving way, both too obstinate to consider the other fellow's point of view.'

James's attitude differed from that of many of his close playing colleagues. He acknowledged Chapman's greatness but would not prostrate himself before the great man. The difference becomes clear when one compares his estimation of George Allison – the man who took over from Chapman – with that of Cliff Bastin.

Bastin subscribed to the school of thought that considered Allison less than proficient where football was concerned and considered that he had simply inherited Chapman's kingdom. James, however, agreed with those who felt Allison had more than matched Chapman by continuing the club's success. Allison, according to James: 'Took over the reins which had been laid down by a man in a million. His task was terribly hard . . . has he failed? The record book gives you the answer. George Allison has triumphed.'

More than that, James preferred Allison's style of management: 'Chapman would put his ideas over in dynamic, forceful, quick-fire ways; Allison gets the same results by friendly, man-to-man co-operation with his players. In my three and a half years under George Allison I never had a single "barney". Which was more than could be said for his relationship with Chapman!

Cliff Bastin, however, was not so whole-hearted in his praise: 'He (Allison) had the name of Arsenal splashed all over the front pages of the press, but he lacked Herbert Chapman's gift of getting the best out of his players.'

Bastin, of course, was a one-club man. He had joined Arsenal as a boy and Chapman had been responsible for 'making' him. Thus, he understandably saw Chapman as being responsible for just about everything that went right at Arsenal, including the 'moulding' of Alex James.

Bastin was always unstinting in his praise of James as a player, but his analysis of how James came to be such a player ran along established 'Svengali-Chapman' lines: at Preston, Bastin wrote, James 'showed signs that he was a real footballer with a first-class constructive brain.' He was, however, 'primarily a dashing goal-scorer, but a shrewd judge of football could detect in some of his touches the presence of exceptional scheming ability'.

James would have had a thing or two to say about that! Showing signs, indeed! And he one of the Wembley Wizards . . .

Bastin and James, in fact, were strangers to one another off the field of play. What Bastin described as James's 'aggressive self-esteem' was never going to prove amenable to 'Boy' Bastin's more conventional character. Bastin was probably Chapman's idea of the model player: modest, utterly respectable and loyal. One imagines Bastin must have winced when watching James's regular rows with the man Bastin once said could have been Prime Minister, had it not been for Chapman's 'lack of opportunities entailed by his position on the social scale'.

Oddly enough, Bastin's explanation for Alex James's off-field shortcomings also centred upon upbringing and social class. Bastin wrote that James:

> was presented with few opportunities. Born in Bellshill, he was never given the advantages of a really thorough education. Thrown out to fight the world unarmed, he struggled through to the top. A magnificent achievement but he might, I feel, have made more of the opportunities which consequently accrued to him had such an education been his.

Unlike Bastin, when James arrived at Arsenal he was an established player, experienced and accomplished; he was also a man impatient with anything pompous, with assumed airs and graces. He enjoyed puncturing inflated egos; rather like his on-field approach, he liked to come at people from odd angles – even people as grand as Herbert Chapman. For instance, while acknowledging that Chapman had a talent where spending large sums of money were concerned, he added:

> Yet with all this huge spending capacity of his, he was

astonishingly 'close' with cash where his own pocket was involved. Call it a streak of eccentricity if you like, but it was a fact that if you went anywhere with Herbert Chapman he would practically always say, 'I haven't brought any money with me. Pay it, will you?'

James, of course, was always keen to tell tales that stood the stereotype of the mean Scotsman on its head; he himself certainly was not tight where money was concerned. He also enjoyed running up expenses for the club to pay, and Chapman annoyed him by refusing to indulge his taste for the extravagant. James would always take a taxi, while Chapman travelled by tube. Chapman was also a stickler for receipts: 'Our most frequent rows were about money. Chapman would try to knock down my expenses and there would be another bust-up.'

Most amusing of all was the running argument the two had over a mysterious 'agent' who was, James claimed, owed £50 for helping with his transfer from Preston to Arsenal. Who this agent was, James never revealed (it could not have been Tom Paton, to whom £50 would have meant nothing.)

I told Chapman that my friend would have to have £50 if I signed for Arsenal and he said, 'Of course, that's all right, I'll see to it.' But when I joined Arsenal and reminded him of the contract he answered, 'I can't put it through yet, Alex. You pay him, and I'll see about it.'

James claims he paid the money – but that Chapman never produced the cash!

But their different attitude towards money reflected different attitudes towards life. James's son recalls:

My father's philosophy was that the world would be a better place if all the people spent their money rather than saved it. Because no way was he going to save any money. He just believed in spending it and thought it would make a happier time for everybody . . .

Arsenal players in general appear to have been very careful with money, and the club, to its credit, set a good example by encouraging its players to save in a special account that offered them extra interest.

Men like David Jack, Charles Buchan, Tom Parker, Cliff Bastin were prudent and sensible. Like Chapman, they were all working-class people who looked to build a better future for themselves and their children; who strove hard to raise their standard of living and to maintain it, and thus to lift themselves on to a higher social plane.

Chapman is said to have considered the happiest day of his life to have been the day his son qualified as a solicitor. Many Arsenal men had bought fine new houses in Finchley, Hendon and Barnet, often with the help of the club, and they endeavoured throughout their careers to use their money wisely. David Jack paid into an insurance policy for the day he would have to give up the game, thus ensuring he had a 'nest egg' to start out on his new life. He had trained for the Civil Service and thus had a profession behind him, and when it came to writing his weekly newspaper column he did it himself, no ghost-writer.

Tom Parker also had a trade to which he would eventually return. He was especially conscious of the opportunity that playing for Arsenal presented him with, for Chapman had obtained him an 'extra' job coaching the boys at a public school. His sons eventually attended the school for free, thus saving considerable expenses while, at the same time, Parker admitted to living off his coaching fees and saving his Arsenal pay whenever he could.

Other Arsenal players were equally frugal, even the unmarried ones. Jack Crayston spent hardly a penny of his wages:

> I was rather mean with myself. My father was a strict man and had always said to me, do what you like but don't spend your money carelessly. Save it. I had five shillings a week spending money and invested the rest in a Building Society. I led a strict life really; I criticise myself, sometimes, but when I went to London I was a bit of a loner. I went to the cinema and the theatres; I didn't isolate myself from the rest of the players but I preferred to have a walk around London and have a cup of tea at a Lyons Corner House. Wilf Copping and I were good mates. We used to wander about in the evenings but generally after a match I'd just walk to the tube and catch a train to Harrow-on-the-Hill, where I had digs. I was lucky there. A family who knew my

family from Grange-over-Sands saw that I was coming to London, and they wrote to my parents offering to put me up. I stayed with them right up until the war.

Crayston may not have been typical of the professional footballer of the period, particularly where the two psalm-books he took with him on his travels were concerned. And yet his teetotal, non-smoking bachelor days were shared by a surprising number of young players; for men like Joe Hulme, Wilf Copping, George Male, the bright lights of the West End held little attraction.

Joe Hulme's great passion as a young man had been billiards, which he played in a local club close by his digs in Stroud Green, within walking distance from Highbury. 'Joe used to sit by the door during the team talks – he'd even have it open, a little, so he could get away fast once it was over and get a table.'

Wilf Copping's extravagance was to wander off from the team hotel and have a quiet Guinness; the majority of the team was teetotal. David Jack's vice was smoking, and so Chapman would arrange for him to have a room of his own when the team travelled.

The club insisted on high standards. Jack Crayston recalls:

> The manager expected you to behave yourself. We were always told that we would be confronted by the press, journalists and so on, and that we were to try and help but not to be controversial. The press could help us and hurt us, we were told. We were also encouraged to confide in the management if we had problems, financial, social, girls; we were like a family. We were friends, how can I put it, in excess of what it says in the dictionary.

And such careful attitudes, such sober life-styles off the pitch, chimed in perfectly with Chapman's philosophy that football held out great possibilities 'for the man who is reasonably careful and lives a decent, straightforward life'.

Footballers, he insisted, were not underpaid and he disagreed with the idea that players ought to be allowed to negotiate individual contracts: 'Some men believe that their value is greater than that of other members of the side and that they are big box-office attractions; but they are dependent on others for their success and they cannot be treated differently.'

Perhaps if players like James had been able to cash in a little more effectively on their undoubted commercial value for endorsing products, the sense of grievance felt might not have been so acute. Advertisers, however, though using sportsmen more and more in the 1930s to help sell their products, rarely offered the men involved more than a token payment.

Arsenal were the supreme side of the decade, and so were featured more than most, but no one in the side appears to have derived any significant extra income from advertisements.

Cigarette manufacturers were especially proficient in using player's images: in an age when nicotine and its dangers were largely unknown or ignored, the sight of a player puffing away caused hardly a ripple of protest. Dixie Dean and Alex Jackson – two matinee idols among footballers – were regularly featured promoting a particular brand and in one such ad Jackson invoked James's name, implying that James too smoked the cigarette. James was paid nothing for this. Neither did he receive any payment from Black Cat Cigarettes when they produced a cigarette card featuring his name and face, and used it prominently in their adverts.

Often players would only find out that they had been used in such a way when the manufacturers sent them something by way of thanks. Dixie Dean recalled that Wix tobacco manufacturers sent him a carton of cigarettes and a £50 cheque out of the blue; Dean gave the cigarettes away, Warny Cresswell, his famous Everton team-mate, crushing them and smoking them in his pipe!

In 1934, Arsenal players were pictured listening to a tiny record printed on the back of a cigarette card – a revolutionary free gift – but they received nothing for their promotional efforts. Tom Parker remembered adverts for Yeastvite, and Rowntree's Gums, Oxo and Phosphorine featuring players from Highbury, but his only recollection of being paid for something was when a wax model of himself was made for Madame Tussaud's after the 1930 Cup Final: 'They gave me £10 for that, and life membership of the museum".

Oxo, Shredded Wheat and Waterman's Pens all thought Arsenal players useful for advertising purposes, but free gifts were all the men received. Bastin tells an amusing story of being approached by the representative of a watch company who wanted him to endorse their product. As a reward he would receive a watch. He dutifully went to tell Chapman, who asked to see the rep. Chapman apparently tore a strip off the man: 'Here is a young man right at the very top of his profession and you mean to tell me you dare offer him a miserable three-guinea watch?'

Well Played, ARSENAL

Here they are in merry mood, elated with the result of their wonderful victory in the presence of His Majesty the King and 92,000 of his loyal subjects. Having footed the ball so skilfully they now show their "hand work" by autographing a ball as a memento of the great occasion. Each member of the team signed with his own Waterman's Pen. All are enthusiastic users of Waterman's.

The ball, together with other sporting mementos, is on view at "The Pen Corner," Kingsway.

No. 52,
27/6, or with
Clip Cap as
shown, 18/6.

If you want a trusty pen, buy Waterman's.
40 Years' Proved Service. Of Stationers,
Jewellers and Stores.

Waterman's

L. G. SLOAN LTD., The Pen Corner, KINGSWAY, LONDON, W.C.2

The man left in a hurry and when he had gone Bastin said to Chapman: 'Thanks very much for looking after me like this, Mr Chapman, but I can't help feeling sorry for that poor fellow who has just gone out.'

Chapman looked up with a twinkle in his eye. 'Well, Cliff, between ourselves, if it had been me, I would have taken the watch right away! But for you, I wanted to get something better . . .'

Manufacturers obtained the services of these young and talented men extremely cheaply – as did the rest of the population. Chapman was not to blame for that, but he bore the brunt of James's frustrations and anger at his inability to make the fortune he considered was rightly his and the two men argued right up until Chapman's death.

Despite the acrimony and the bluster, a mutual respect endured to the very end; a mutual respect shared by the two men whose great careers would always remain indissolubly linked.

17

Veteran Years

I knew, or thought I knew, that if Arsenal lost this match it would be the finish of Alex James.   Alex James in the *News of the World*, 1937

TWO MONTHS AFTER Herbert Chapman died, Alex James received another shock. Joe Shaw, assistant manager at Arsenal, called him into the office one morning in March 1933 and told him that Derby County wanted to buy him – and that Arsenal was prepared to let him go.

Derby had offered Arsenal two England internationals, Cooper and Crooks, for much-needed cash. The new Arsenal manager, George Allison, had offered cash – and James. His value had been put at about £2,000.

It was a moment of truth for both Arsenal and James. Allison was faced with the difficult job of restructuring the team that Chapman had so rightly said was 'played out'. Its struggle to retain the League title was faltering and the last 10 games had resulted in just four wins, four draws and two defeats. Players such as Bob John, Charlie Jones, David Jack and Jack Lambert were approaching the ends of their careers: James, Allison thought, was another of them.

Derby was understandably keen to acquire him. The manager, George Jobey, was a close friend of James's and the club trainer was James's father-in-law, Dave Willis. James, however, was in no mood to bargain seriously. 'Listen, Joe, I said, if Arsenal wants to get rid of me or wants to kick me out, all right, I'll go. But I'm going only if I receive all the money that Derby hands over for my transfer.'

Promises of jobs in the town and a nice house fell on deaf ears. James felt that he could make more money outside football if he remained in London; besides, he had helped build Arsenal into what it was. It was a matter of pride.

THE STORY OF ALEX JAMES

See Page 7

PEARSON'S WEEKLY

No. 2317   Registered For Transmission to Canada.   **WEEK ENDING DECEMBER 22, 1934**   PRICE 2d.

As it turned out, his decision to stand firm was a good one, both for himself and for the club. He had regained his place in the side the week before the transfer offer, at almost the same time that Ted Drake made his debut. Together, they rejuvenated the Arsenal attack, and Arsenal won nine of the last 11 games – and took the title for the second successive season.

The following season, as Allison continued with his rebuilding, James remained in possession of the inside left position and became the master-mind of a 'new' Arsenal championship-winning side. Regulars such as Bastin, Roberts, Male and Hapgood continued, but new men such as Copping and Crayston, Bowden, Davidson and Drake added youth and strength to Chapman's original side.

James played in 30 League matches, 29 of them alongside Drake, the new scoring sensation. This was the partnership Bill Shankly recalled many years later:

James was a genius. He would put Vaseline on his face and had a cocky countenance. He was a master player who just oozed confidence . . . it was a nightmare playing against them. James was picking the ball up in midfield and poking it here and there. He would say to Ted Drake, 'Right, up, Ted!'

Ted got the ball just outside the box and hit it. If our goalkeeper had got his hands to it it would have taken them off. Dear God, that shot was frightening.

Drake scored 42 goals in 41 matches. He was the new Dixie Dean and it was largely his goals that saw Arsenal to their third championship.

For James, the arrival of Wilf Copping at left half was just as important a factor in his success in holding a place in the first team. Copping gained a reputation as an iron man. Bill Shankly recalled a clash in the 1938 England–Scotland match:

The grass was short, the ground was quick and I was playing the ball. The next thing I knew, Copping had done me down the front of my right leg. He had burst the stocking – the shin pad was out – and cut my leg. That was after 10 minutes and it was my first impression of Copping. He didn't need to be playing at home to kick you – he would have kicked you in your own back yard or in your own chair . . .

In the FA Cup in 1936, Grimsby Town's inside forward Jackie Bestall was deputed to 'shadow' James: 'but nobody had bothered to tell me about Wilf Copping playing behind Alex. I was either on my back or falling!'

Copping's great partner and room-mate, Jack Crayston, thought him

tough, but not dirty. He often carried an injury sustained during a match without complaining. He broke his nose once and continued, just said it hurt a bit! He was courageous. He had a broad Yorkshire accent but he was quiet – a tough egg! Not a conversationalist. On match days he wouldn't shave – I think he thought it made him look more fearsome.

James would play more or less between us. If we got the ball we automatically looked for him. As captain, he did things in a quiet way, he didn't gesticulate. He didn't ask for the ball, just put himself in a position where he could receive it. We were all amazed at his ability. I was a physically strong player but I never fouled with the intention of doing so – that's why they called me 'Gentleman Jack'.

We were a defensive side, if you like. We would fall back leaving Ted and the two wingers up – but we'd break out together. I scored 12 goals one season. Often, I would act as a decoy for Ted Drake in the penalty area at corners, because I was tall. Wilf and I were complete opposites – maybe that was why we got on so well.

To combat James, even though he was now at the veteran stage of his career, was still a nightmare for the opposition: whichever way the tactics were shaped, they seemed to backfire.

In 1931, when closing a series of reminiscences, James had written: 'What of my future? Maybe I'll yet live to score a hat trick. I've never been guilty of that in my whole career.'

Yet, in the middle of the triple championship season, 1934/35, that most unlikely of things happened: on 2 February at Highbury against Sheffield Wednesday James scored that hat trick. How he managed it – or rather, why – is part of Highbury folklore and typical of the furore that surrounded just about everything he did. Wednesday's manager, Billy Walker, is supposed to have told his players not to mark James near the Wednesday area because 'he never scores these days'. Another version of the story current for many years gave his son the credit for having goaded his father by coming home on the morning of the match after scoring seven goals in a school match, and wondering why he, the great Alex James, never did the same.

Two years after the event, however, James provided a clue as to his frame of mind that afternoon. He recalled that the day before the game, manager Allison had signed Bobby Davidson from St Johnstone, a stocky little inside forward whom Allison declared, rather oddly to have, 'a big sweeping mind and feet to respond to it'. He was apparently, the 'new Alex James'.

It was freely circulated that after I had scored the hat trick against Sheffield Wednesday I went into the dressing-room at the finish and said, 'That'll teach them to sign anybody in my place.'. . .

[This James declared, was a 'wicked untruth'.] . . . It was a rotten yarn but it stuck and, incredibly enough, even some of the Arsenal players believed it. In fact, I'm not at all sure that Bobby himself did not think there was something in it.

In fact, the last couple of seasons, success-filled though they were, caused James a great deal of heart-searching. With each match he grew less and less able to cope with injuries; he was approaching his middle thirties: someone would have to 'replace him' at some point. (Although Davidson would, like many others, turn out not to be the man and would be transferred to Newcastle in November 1937.)

Insecurity dogged him, and he did not make things any easier for himself. The season of 1935/36 saw the side badly hit by injuries; the League title for a fourth year was clearly not a possibility. James himself played only 10 games before Christmas, his form and fitness suffering. When the Cup ties came around again, he was, he declared, under a bit of a cloud:

Money troubles were worrying me a lot and my game suffered accordingly. It is no use anyone telling me that once you are on the field with 50,000 people yelling, and the game waiting to be played, you forget everything except the job in hand. It doesn't work.

Tottenham Hotspur Football & Athletic Company, Limited.

Official Programme

And Record of the Club.

Issued every Match Day.

PRICE ONE PENNY.

Vol. XXVII. No. 41.

MARCH 6, 1935.

C. Coventry, Trade Union Printer, Lower Tottenham.

James could not concentrate and he was left out of the side that began the season's Cup campaign by winning an away match against Bristol Rovers. On this occasion, Allison and Whittaker were at odds regarding the best forward line-up. When Bristol (a Third Division side) went into the lead by a goal to nil, and were clearly on top, Whittaker, though ostensibly only the team trainer, locked himself and the team in the dressing-room at half-time – without Allison. After giving the team a dressing-down, he moved Davidson from inside left and Bastin took on the 'James' role. The team went out in the second half and won.

In the next round, for which Arsenal was drawn against Liverpool at Anfield, James sensed a reprieve in the air:

> No announcement was made but I travelled up with them. 'The team will be chosen shortly before kick-off,' Mr Allison told us. I don't know why, but somehow I sensed that I would be given one last chance to see if I could hit form again.

He was right. Allison, influenced by Whittaker, decided to play him and James admitted:

> I have never had many nervous moments in football but I confess here and now that I was in an awful state before the Cup tie. I knew, or thought I knew, that if Arsenal lost this match it would be the finish of Alex James.

Arsenal won 2-0 and James had made another 'come-back'. He remained in the side for the remainder of the Cup campaign and led Arsenal (so badly hit by injuries all season that, in 'rationing' their players' appearances for crucial games, they incurred fines by the FA for fielding weak teams) to the Cup Final where they met Second Division Sheffield United. For that momentous occasion, he was made captain.

It was a poor final, a 'war of attrition' with Sheffield on top, although Arsenal's 'Operation Quick Goal' at the opening of the second half nearly caused a scoring sensation akin to James's winning strike back in 1930.

In a pre-arranged move, James held the ball while Crayston raced forward into the penalty area: James sent through a perfect pass which Crayston hit first time – only for United's goalkeeper Smith

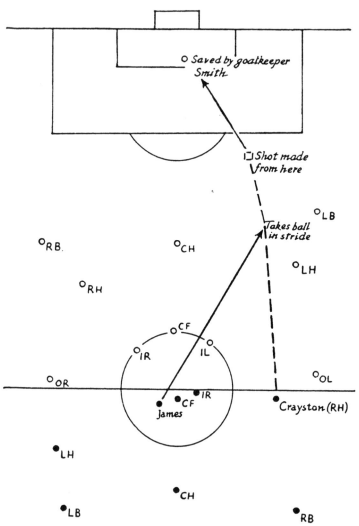

O Saved by goalkeeper
Smith

Shot made
from here

Takes ball
in stride

○LB

○RB.   ○CH

                                    ○LH

○RH

                ○CF
        ○IR   ○ IL

○OR   ○OL

        ●CF ●IR
    James   ●Crayston (RH)

●LH

                ●CH

    ●LB   ●RB

Kick-off move by Arsenal in the 1936 F.A. Cup Final against Sheffield
United. The ball was kicked off to the inside-right who pushed it back
and to the left. James chipped the ball into the gap between the centre-
half and left-back, where it was taken by Crayston, who set off at top
speed at the kick-off.

to pull off a tremendous save. In the 74th minute, however, Arsenal scored:

> Alec slipped the ball along the line to Cliff Bastin who, in an instant, squared it to the fast-moving Drake. Ted, with Johnson breathing down his neck and Alex yelling 'It's all yours, Ted,' went one way, came back again and hit a beautiful left-foot shot past the diving Smith into the net.

Thus, James lifted the Cup and, as he put it a year later:

> When I saw George Allison about re-signing for the following season I had few qualms for the future. After all, hadn't I, an old-timer said to be worn out and finished, come back and led the team to win the Cup?

It was obvious that 1936/37 was going to be his last season, but he wanted to be sure that he would be considered for the first team. Chapman had once said that veteran players would never be just ditched; that they would be signed on for a season, at least, in order that they could sort out their affairs and still be paid. But James wanted no favours:

> Besides, I fancied I could make more money outside the game if I left at that time while my name was on everybody's tongue. It was no use to me to sink gradually into the reserves and from there into oblivion. I wanted to cash in on my name while it was still of some value.

The same season that James captained Arsenal in the Cup Final, his old school-mate Hughie Gallacher led Derby County to take second place in the First Division. Their careers were thus reaching a joint climax; in fact they could have ended their playing days together, for eight months after failing to persuade James to join them, Derby County succeeded in attracting Gallacher from Chelsea for £3,000.

Gallacher's career had come to a standstill in London and Derby was seen as a new start for him. The club helped him pay off various outstanding debts and he made it known that he intended to reform – no drinking, a settled existence.

He repaid Derby with 38 goals in 52 games. But his two-year

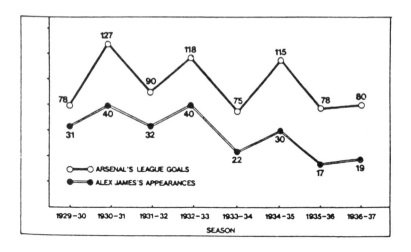

This graph shows the remarkable correlation between Alex James's Football League appearances and Arsenal's goals. It appears in
The Book of Football by Norman Barrett, published by Purnell

spell with the Rams was to be his last significant contribution to First Division football. The following season, in 1937, he joined Notts County in the Third Division South. He still scored goals, but he had stepped out of the limelight.

His compensation – with James at Arsenal still taking League and Cup medals – was that his Scotland career had continued until 1935, and though he had had to wait four years while arguments between the Scottish FA and the English authorities had bedevilled selection for all the national teams, his two final matches were to be against the Old Enemy. In 1934 he played at Wembley when England won 2-0 but, in 1935, he went out on a deserved high note when Scotland beat England 3-0 at Hampden before a massive crowd of over 120,000.

James had had no such send-off. He had received his recall some two years earlier than Gallacher in October 1932, and had been on the wrong end of a second 5-2 defeat, this time by the Welsh. In April 1933 he had been selected for the match against England but, as John Rafferty put it, 'Alec James was chosen to play but called off on the Tuesday before the match, saying he was unfit. He played, however, for Arsenal on the Saturday and made himself an outcast. He had let the colours down.' James was never selected again.

The international had come at a crucial time for Arsenal. The second League title had seemed to be slipping away; the team had won just one of its previous eight games and Aston Villa, the opponent on that fateful April afternoon, were catching up fast. James was playing well for Arsenal in the middle of the longest unbroken run of appearances he would ever make in League football. It was a hard choice. That he turned out for Arsenal was made the harder to bear in Scotland by the fact that his team-mate Joe Hulme decided to play for England. Scotland won 2-1. Arsenal won 5-0, the start of a five-victory sequence that would take it clear of all opponents.

In a sense, it had been a declaration of loyalties that James had long since decided upon. His international career spanning seven years but consisting of just eight caps may seem a modest one, even for the time, but for most of it he had been playing amongst giants such as Morton, Jackson, McMullen and Gallacher. It was hard of the Scots to condemn him at the end; typical that Gallacher should have been taken to their hearts as a truer son. For James had contributed, in true Scottish style, to one of the greatest club sides the world had seen, the most innovative of the era eclipsing even the great Rangers sides of the 1930s. As one of the most progressive players in the game's long history he had kept the flag of Scottish football flying; certainly his contribution to that most English of sides (with due apologies to the Welshmen involved), Arsenal F.C. was the crucial one.

James was never one to wax sentimental, however. If he had offended, then the fault was not his. Even in 1931 he had been prepared to have a joke at the Scottish Football Association's expense. Commenting on being capped three times by Scotland he said:

That's not strictly accurate for, though I played in three internationals, I received only one cap. The embroidery on it says: 1929/30 v. Wales v. Ireland v. England. Some of the boys think it a great joke the way the Scottish Football Association makes one cap do the work of three!

Neither on the field nor off it was James a fervent nationalist 'bore'; his children recall visiting Scotland rarely, even after his playing days were over. Patsy recalls:

Even then we only went once in a while. A relative's wedding, I remember – and on the way up, we went to both Mum and Dad's birthplace and Dad's was just a sort of slag-heap. The Buildings had been torn down, I think. He didn't make much of his Scottish background, except on Hogmanay and he wasn't one for going back to his 'roots'. There were the obvious things about him that never changed though: his accent, for a start, which was very thick. The people next door in Barnet couldn't understand him at all. They would say yes and no and hoped they'd said it in the right order! And he always had a thing about Catholics – a school-friend of mine wore a crucifix and he once asked her why she was wearing 'that pitch and toss'. He liked rhyming slang, Cockney slang, though he hated my 'London' accent. 'I'm paying for her to go to private school and it's costing me a fortune, and she still talks like a Cockney!' he would complain.

He returned to Scotland now and then to visit his sisters who were still living in Bellshill. He would arrive suddenly, the famous brother, unheralded, bearing gifts. Jim Murdoch, son of James's sister Mary, remembers his mother complaining, 'He's just in and out, once around the table and a kick at the cat, that was as much as you saw of him!' Chrissie, his other sister remembered: 'He would just arrive at the back door: "Hullo Chrissie!" he'd say and I would say "You stay here just long enough to wash your hands and then you're off again . . ."

He enjoyed bringing them expensive presents: one Christmas, Chrissie's son Alex received a complete Hornby train set, some-thing that even in those days cost a great deal.

Yet he would stay with no one; he would book into a small pub-cum-hotel at Woodend, just across the railway line from where the Buildings had once stood. It was a depressing little place but, then, it matched Bellshill. The village had continued to decline throughout the 1930s, its inhabitants, in George Orwell's phrase, 'settling down to unemployment'. Many families had moved south, following the local steel works as they set up plants in Corby in Northamptonshire. For those who remained, it was working in allotments, keeping chickens, blackberrying or mushrooming in late summer or scrabbling on the coal-tips or pilfering from coal-yards and railway wagons. The view from Woodend along the bleak main street of Bellshill must have been a sad one.

London more than ever was Alex James's world now: Barnet his home. He had made an uneasy transition, full of contradictions, many of which remained unresolved. His sense of social dislocation was epitomised by the decision to put both his children into private schools. Patsy remembers:

It was difficult for Mum and Dad. All the children where we lived went to private schools. I suppose they were trying to do the best for us but Alec, my brother, always had a thing about it, resented it, and he found it harder than me.

Alec remembered the school as being a small institution:

It was a lot easier to start up a little school in those days. Ours just had five or six boys and about seven girls. It was only a hundred yards up the road from where we lived in Barnet. We all had to wear a blue blazer, proper little uniforms which must have cost a bit. Perhaps that was why the old man liked the idea, because he was a hell of a one for being presentable. You had to have a clean shirt, you had to have your shoes highly polished. I used to think the only thing he did besides play football was polish his bloody shoes!

I went to a paid grammar school, too, because Dad had this idea that the reason I'd failed the eleven plus was because they knew he could afford to pay for my education (or they thought he could) so why should I go to a state school, that sort of thing. I was there till I was 15.

The private school, however, was just one aspect of life for the son and daughter of a man who seemed to enjoy living in the spotlight:

I think Alec was embarrassed by his father's nature, the fuss that was always made. He was a more sensitive sort of boy – yet on the face of it he had what every boy must have dreamed of! Going to the Arsenal ground whenever he liked, into the dressing-rooms; treated on the treatment table by Tom Whittaker; meeting all the players.

But he lived in my shadow a bit, I think. Because I *was* a pain! I was the show-off, loved to be in the forefront of everything. If players came round in the evening to play cards I'd wake up and

hear them and I'd deck myself out in something and float into
the room and stand on my head! They'd all say, 'Let her stay up!'
and I'd play about, coquettish, a little madam. In the morning I
would wake up and there would be players dossing down on the
floor, on the settee. It was a home from home for some of them.

The James household, in fact, in contrast to the respectable sur-
burbia all around, was a merry place. Alec recalls:

My father was always keen for the younger players to come back
home – we had a sort of open house, if you like. When you were
new to a club, living in digs, especially if you were from the north,
it could be a little bit lonely. You would miss the home cooking,
and Mum was from Newcastle and a good cook and so Dad would
just invite players back. 'Tell Peggy to cook you a meal.' Ted
Drake remembers being taken back and Alex saying, 'Cook old
Ted a steak!' And Mum enjoyed it all, liked to entertain. It was
company for her, and she liked to laugh and have a party. The
young boys would act as baby-sitters, too, looking after us when
Mum and Dad went out for the evening. The younger boys could
bring their girl-friends back, play records; Pat Beasley, Denis
Compton, Frank Hill . . .

Mum had chosen the house in Barnet (Arsenal bought it and
they paid a nominal rent) especially because it had a through-
lounge, which was unusual then. You could just roll the carpet
back and dance. It was a friendly place for players to go when
they had time on their hands, better than wandering off to the
dog-track. I would say mother had as much to do with the good
relationship among players at the club, the good atmosphere, as
anyone else.

As kids, we were roped into Dad's routine. It was like clockwork. He would be down at the ground by 10, for training, and
then home in the afternoon for a round of golf. Then it would be
out to the cinema and we'd all go. Always Finsbury Park Empire
on a Friday night because the manager welcomed Arsenal players
– the front three rows were free.

Dad liked all the American films – hated the British ones. And
his favourite was Jimmy Cagney: he thought he was fantastic. I
supposed he dressed a bit like him!

It was difficult to get much homework done, really, because

Goodbye to Arsenal, James shakes hands with Crayston, while Milne and Davidson look on

James enjoyed turning out for the occasional charity game; above he is seated next to a balding Hughie Gallacher, while below he enjoys a joke with Denis Compton (left) and Tommy Lawton before going into action. (Keystone)

we would go to the cinema sometimes five times a week. Not that we were complaining, but we knew every cinema in north London intimately. It was always a job on a Sunday to find something we hadn't been to and we'd end up going to see a B-feature or a foreign film . . .

I spent a lot of my youth either sitting in Dad's car outside Joe Bloomfield's bar in Leicester Square or at Joe Branelly's house, listening to American records which Branelly was adapting for Ambrose's orchestra, or maybe pinching the arrangements from! All the band-boys loved Dad. We've been at the Palladium when they've spotted Dad three rows back and more or less stopped the show to say, 'Good luck on Saturday.' I would be taken backstage to meet people, famous variety stars who, through their make-up, would be telling me what a great man my father was. I remember watching Len Harvey training for a championship at Whetstone, and Benny Lynch was often at our house. Dad had to go and find him sometimes when he was on a 'bender' and supposed to be training for a fight, have to go and search all the nightclubs and drag him back. Billy Cotton, the Crazy Gang – we would meet so many people and they all wanted to shake Dad's hand.

But I was the wrong sort of personality. It was a sort of pressure, right from when I was four years old: 'I suppose you're going to be a footballer like your father?'

Maybe, if I'd gone to a state school I'd have kicked a ball more often early on, but at the little junior school we went to I wasn't allowed to. 'You might get your knees dirty, you must keep your shirt clean' – that sort of thing. It was a constant conflict. I did go to the park with some stumps when I could, and I played with Dad in the garden and on the beach and tried to work out what it was he did. I remember he was always making little sounds, little noises that would put you off – you couldn't appreciate that, that a gesture, or a sound, could throw you off balance and trick you. And he was full of tricks!

For Alec junior, it proved hard to find common ground with a man regarded as the greatest footballer in the world. He was effusive, generous and kind and yet always something of a stranger:

I could never play him at cards. I never liked them anyway, but with him it was impossible! I suppose with all the time they had on their hands they got pretty good at it. He could sit there on his own with four hands and memorise each card, so that you could never hope to win . . .

It is no surprise that the children's regular holidays to Derby to stay with their grandparents were much looked forward to. Patsy remembers that:

Some of my happiest memories were on holiday there in their little bungalow. It was called Raith and painted black and white – Newcastle's colours! There was a photograph in the hallway of Daddy being presented to the Prince of Wales: he's shaking hands, but he's grinning into the camera. That was just Daddy. He's supposed to have done it for a bet but he might have made that tale up . . .

I suppose we didn't have to live up to Daddy there, with our grandparents. Not so much pressure. We used to enjoy going to Derby's ground. We supported them more than Arsenal! There was something different about it, more homely, than Highbury, though Derby had some great players then: Sammy Crooks and Raich Carter. I would go along with Grandma to the match, after Alec had gone along earlier with Grandad. Grandma never used to swear at all but on Saturday afternoons she was raring to go! While, at Arsenal, Mum never went to a match. That was one thing Dad always said he agreed with Herbert Chapman about; they didn't think women should go to football matches!

At Derby, you see, Alec could travel with the kit, with Grandad and they would let him sit on the trainer's bench, that sort of thing, whereas at Arsenal it was all rather remote. He had a seat in the new stand, but that isn't what a youngster really likes is it?

At home it was either terrific highs or terrific lows. It could be exciting when Mum and Dad were going out to a function; we would be getting ready for bed while Mum was in an evening gown and Dad was in tails; but then things could go wrong suddenly. He was a very private man in many ways – a bit of a lone wolf. You couldn't really rely on him, yet he would surprise you. I asked him to come to my school one day to start the school races on Sports Day. He wasn't a great one for that sort of thing and he made an excuse and didn't come. And I found out later that he had been playing golf. He was just like that: he wouldn't think that you would be upset, he just did what he wanted to do. Yet he made such a fuss of us in other ways and was so generous. When they won the Cup in 1936, it was one of the happiest days of his life, I think. The lady next door was very ill with cancer and he just took the Cup round with champagne and we all drank out of it! It was such a day – and that was just like him. If you'd asked him, he might not have done it.

But the life-style with long lazy holidays in the West Country, a new car each year, the best clothes from the best tailors, though it may have matched that of his neighbours in Barnet, was built on rapidly shifting sand. Alex's spending habits meant that at the end of each season, he had little more in the bank that what he had started with.

The last few seasons had been so worrying for him because he knew that his 'image' was going to be all that he could sell: he had no trade, and no investments. It was going to be his name standing between his present life and a rather less glamorous one. And this he compounded by his determination not to go into football management: 'I'm not going to get bloody ulcers,' he told his son.

The alternative was 'business', something that Alex James was probably the least well-equipped footballer in the British Isles to succeed in. But, as he said goodbye to Arsenal in June 1937, his hopes were high: his future, he announced to readers of the *News of the World*, was secure.

18

Cashing In At Last

Put yourself in the position of a man who has been earning £400 a year and more, who has a wife and children and who suddenly finds himself on the list of the unemployed. The bottom has dropped out of his world. He feels he must do something to make a fresh start and, perhaps without proper advice, he plunges into an undertaking which fails. Such a man deserves pity.

Herbert Chapman, *Herbert Chapman on Football*, 1934

ALEX JAMES PLAYED his last competitive match for Arsenal in Holland at the Feyenoord Stadium in Rotterdam on 6 June 1937 – ironic when one recalls how adamant he had always been about not playing 'extra' matches.

He had missed Arsenal's only other close-season tour during his career at Highbury (in 1931) and had regularly been absent, for one reason or another, whenever Arsenal had played extra 'prestige' matches. He had missed all three Charity Shield matches; three of the five fixtures with Glasgow Rangers (a regular, unofficial British Championship which Rangers invariably won); and five of the eight games against Racing Club of Paris (another regular fixture, this time in aid of disabled First World War soldiers).

On the Scandinavian tour of 1937, by contrast, he played in all but one of the matches – an indication of how keenly he felt he was going to miss the game once he had hung up his boots.

As he wrote a few months later in opening his *News of the World* story: 'I would give anything I possess to be able to put back the clock and return to the days when I was starting my career in the game.'

His imminent retirement from football had, however, appeared to cause him no sleepless nights. He had set his face against football management and, instead, decided that exploiting his image would be the key to a profitable future.

There had, however, been ominous pointers as to how that future 'career' might go. The sweet and tobacco shop bearing his name, opposite the Finsbury Park Empire, just a short walk from Highbury Stadium, had been his first 'business' venture. Shops of this nature had long been popular with footballers as somewhere to invest their nest-eggs safely. Unfortunately, the James venture had been doomed from the very start. According to Patsy:

He appeared to have bought the shop in an off-hand moment. A woman – we never found out who – asked him if he was interested and he just handed over the cash, so many hundreds of pounds. Then he came home and said, 'I've bought a sweet-shop.' Mum wasn't pleased at all. She had no idea how to run a shop. And then it turned out that it hadn't been the woman's to sell in the first place; she owned it with her husband and, of course, Dad had no receipt, which was typical.

It was a strain for Mum to have to go down to this little shop, which really did hardly any business at all. The crowd passing on the way to a match each fortnight brought in some trade but you could only get two or three in at any one time and one of them was usually there just to see Alex James. And he was never there. The girl who eventually ran it for us used to say, 'You've just missed him!'

He would occasionally call in and pick up a packet of cigarettes with his friends before popping across to the Finsbury Park Empire for a drink . . .

Eventually, the local council discovered that there was no toilet there for the girl. She had an arrangement that she could pop across to the theatre when she needed to, but she told this to the Sanitary Inspector in all innocence and they immediately insisted that one was installed. Dad just got rid of the place after that, because it wasn't worth the expense. We enjoyed it as kids, of course; a sweet-shop! But it really was a waste of money.

In June 1937, however, James was busily preparing for a career that would, he hoped, be launched on the back of maximum publicity derived from a provocative and apparently scandalous series of 'memoirs' to be published in the *News of the World*.

During the summer it was announced that James was 'somewhere in Devon', working hard on his memoirs. 'Now that I am out

FOOTBALL—With the Lid Off!
by ALEX JAMES
FAMOUS SCOTTISH INTERNATIONAL & ARSENAL FORWARD

Specially illustrated for the "News of the World" by CYRIL HOLLOWAY.

"THE TRUTH of the 'RACKET' MUST BE TOLD"

T O-DAY we begin publication of the reminiscences of one of the greatest Association footballers of all time.

To the universal regret of uncounted thousands, Alex James, the diminutive but indomitable and incomparable Scottish and Arsenal forward, has finished his career on the professional field.

It has lasted for fifteen exciting years—exciting not in the playing sense alone, but for the countless occasions upon which, sometimes deliberately, sometimes unwittingly, he became the central figure in hectic little battles in the board room.

Alex James makes no secret of the fact that he was in commercialised football for every penny honestly to be won from it, and because of that determination encountered more stormy weather than meets the average professional.

In these reminiscences, therefore, he proposes to write generally on the games of other years, but more particularly of the subterfuge, the conspiracy, the plotting and the palaver which beset the life of a star player.

¶ That is why he has christened his amazing revelations "Football—With the Lid Off!"

M Y boots are hanging by their laces to a clothes-peg. I have kicked a football for the last time.

Fifteen years in the game. What years they have been! I have met some of the grandest fellows in the world, and I have seen some of the worst.

Football has been my life. If I had the chance to live that life over again I would be—just a footballer!

That is how I feel about it. I have only one regret. To be able to put back the clock and return to the days when I was starting my decision. It is a lot I could have done, there is even more that I want to do, but I feel, any day, I...

You see, the place where I was born, Mossend, is a little village surrounded by other industrial places—Belishill, Holytown and Mossend, near Glasgow. All the folk ate short. All the folk are football barmy.

Have you ever played in bare feet? We used to as often as not, when a couple of teams were going to play each other on a Saturday we had no boots at all, and, so that there should be no unfair advantage about that, those who had boots agreed to take them off, and we'd all play in our bare feet.

My School Pal Hughie

E VERY mad of Mossend was daft about football, but there were two outstanding. They were my own self and the other was a lad who went to the same school—Hughie Gallacher.

Hughie and I hit it off right from the "off" (played truant) from school together, and we romped in the streets together.

Many an hour Hughie and I spent with a ball in one of the streets and on the field at the back of the streets...

I was choosen for a Belishill juvenile team, and—since that meant I could play in a local tourney, and Hughie, who was away at the time, played for Belishill Athletic was just about the best thing on the juvenile scene. So I thought they were certain to take me out of the Brandon Amateurs and make me a member of their team.

But they didn't. Nothing would convince the Athletic's selectors to play in their class of football.

Discretion Before Valour

S TILL, my break came. I played for Brandon in a match against Orbiston Celtic. I must have done something during that game, for Rangers, Orbiston's "tough guy," came up and said he would see I did not play for any more matches that season.

Well, I wanted him out but made an order...

Orbiston itself was just a couple of rows of miners' houses and a football field with a wooden stand in it, and about a thousand spectators, but something happened which set my future in the game. Suddenly there was honour in the game.

Tommy Rogers, who, as I have told you, was known in the sport as a tough boy, took me under his wing. Rogers could not have been kinder had I been a visiting player or something like me.

My honour had made it his job to look after me, and he certainly did it.

Be at the game, if I was to get on well lightly. Everytime I got my foot to the ball, there he was near me. When someone thundered at me when I had at that time, the name being quite a protection...

The result of all this—protection was that I could play my own style of football without having much to worry about. And gradually the word got bumped off the ball...

"Alex, I want you to come along and play for my second eleven," I said I could.

Then Mr. Hunter suggested that I should go down to the Motherwell works, getting on top of a world I bit of training. I thought that sounded...

I went on the Monday night after work, feeling on top of the ground and watched during practice.

"That is the life for me!" I thought, and I said along and told me what to do along and told me what to do...

Nobody took the slightest notice of me. I could always get about it all more annoyed about it all until I could see anything.

Some time afterwards I met Sailor Hunter. "You're a fine fellow!" he said. "Why didn't you come down for training that time we arranged to set that ground for an hour writing in that you? Everybody there...

Stepping Up the Ladder

I T was at Ashfield that my first honour came. I was chosen to play for Glasgow Junior Loafer against Midlothian.

That in itself was wonderful to me, but even more exciting was the news that later the Raith Rovers, Motherwell, and Plymouth Argyle had representatives there.

This was my very first grand game before me all those early years. I loved...

THE PLAYERS LAUGHED AT HUGHIE AND SAID: "YOU WANT TO SEE YOU TWO! YOU COUPLE OF SHRIMPS!"—"I'M TOO WEE!"

They were a great side, but I didn't want to help them much.

FROM ONE JOB TO ANOTHER

of football I can tell all those things which have had to be hushed up. My story is a frank and open confession. I have an idea that it is going to startle the football world.'

And from the very first article entitled: 'Football With The Lid Off – The truth of the Racket must be told!' it seemed that he was going to tear aside the cloak of respectability that had been drawn across the deceitful mess of football's finances. That the series fell some way short of the extravagant claims must not detract from their startling nature: startling for the time and the context.

Football 'life stories' were usually little more than old newspaper cuttings of significant football matches stitched together by a journalist who would spice the whole thing with various personal quips, comments and observations contributed by the ostensible author – though sometimes even these were concocted by the hack. James himself had had at least three such stories published under his name already.

The *News of the World* series was different because, although he named few names (the law of libel would have prevented that), he talked of matters normally considered too 'dangerous' for mere players to mention in print.

Everyone knew – or thought they knew – that clubs offered players and managers and event agents substantial bribes for the signatures of wanted men; but for the first time James talked freely about demands for under-the-counter money, of illegal offers, of agents. That he stopped short of admitting that he had accepted sums of money made little difference. (More often, it would seem, he was refused money that he had demanded!) The tone of the memoirs was typical of the man, cocking a snook disrespectfully at pompous officialdom in risqué fashion, and no one got away. Referees, directors, managers, League officials: none escaped some sort of censure. Even that apparently untouchable edifice, Herbert Chapman, was presented in a less than perfect light.

In a way, the memoirs were more a confession than an accusation, however, and at the very start it was stated: 'Alex James makes no secret of the fact that he was in commercialised football for every penny honestly to be won from it'. It was this openness that rendered him less than attractive in the eyes of football's officials. In today's terminology, James could be said to have 'brought the game into disrepute'.

But he was only bringing to a dramatic climax an attitude he had adopted throughout his career: that money was not something to be ashamed of; that a society which regarded questions about one's personal income and savings as somehow indecent was not his sort of society.

It is no coincidence that James's hero was James Cagney, the pint-sized, immaculately dressed little scrapper, wise-cracking his way to the top of the heap, justifying any apparent illegalities by pointing to the hypocrisy of the 'respectable' people who made the rules. James certainly liked to see himself as an 'Angel With A Dirty Face', and the illustrations accompanying the life story (James dashing here, accusing there, trilby pulled down over his eyes, well-cut suit hugging a powerful body) could have come straight from a Hollywood publicity department.

The FA would take no action against him; they had no need. James had ensured his ultimate banishment from the game by simultaneously announcing at the beginning of his life story that he was going to take up 'an important position with a football pools firm'. Large adverts announcing Ring Pools appeared with James's face prominently displayed over them, urging potential punters to write to him. Patsy recollects that:

> We were going to make our fortunes . . . we were going to be millionaires. We never met the other people involved, but I do remember our garage was so full of pools coupons that we couldn't park the car.
>
> Lots of celebrities and film-stars lent their names to pools advertising in those days – mainly, they would present the cheques. It was a way of earning some quick money. I don't think Dad invested that much, but he was a director and so he was liable for any losses or if they went bankrupt. He was drawing a wage of anything between £15 to £40 a week. Unfortunately, it didn't last very long.

The football pools were a social phenomenon of the 1930s. There had long been fixed-odds betting on football results: bookmakers issued coupons and paid out a certain amount if a successful prediction was made of a combination of home wins, away wins and drawn games. But the abuses of the system, the fixing of results, the bribing of players, the syndicates, made the football authorities wary of, not to say hostile towards, the whole business. Footballers, needless to say, were ordered to have nothing to do with them.

By the 1930s, however, the modern football 'pool' had come into existence: a much safer system, not tied to bookmakers, which involved paying out variable sums each week according to a participant's success in predicting a set number of draws across the whole of the Football League fixture list. Thus, trying to fix this or that match was rendered futile; the size of the winnings depended on the number of people participating – the more bets, the bigger the pool to be shared out.

The FA remained opposed to the whole concept and would thus fail to benefit financially until the 1950s. In 1933, the League attempted to prevent the pools companies from using their fixture lists, which they claimed were copyright, but they failed, along with parliamentary attempts to abolish pools betting. The pools idea was simply too popular: it was also fair and exciting, and thus continued to grow.

By 1936 it was estimated that between five and seven million people were paying three shillings (15p) a week on average; that 30 million pounds was being gambled each year. With so much money at stake, scores of smaller firms entered the fray. Few survived for long, however; the competition was intense and the overheads were surprisingly high: postage, printing, staff to lick the stamps and check the entries, renting of office space and, above all, advertising.

During the 1930s the big companies – Sangsters, Littlewoods, Copes – spent heavily on advertising. Littlewoods even invested in a purpose-built building for more effective processing of coupons. The economies of size worked aggressively in their favour. The bigger the company, the bigger the prize, and that was publicity enough.

Alex James and Ring Pools never really stood a chance. It was a venture floated by various interested parties based at that famous boxing venue, the Ring in Blackfriars. James had moved in boxing circles for many years: Joe Bloomfield's was, after all, one of his favourite watering-holes. He had also earned occasional pocket money appearing on stage with light-heavyweight champion and would-be crooner Eddie Phillips in a celebrity double-act of gags and practical demonstrations.

But it was clear that the syndicate had invested little by way of working capital. Much of the impetus for the launch rested on

The advertisement for Ring Pools which appeared in the *News of the World* during the summer of 1937

James's name and its ability to bring in people willing to gamble. On 5 September, just a month after the company began, James was pictured in the *News of the World* presenting a modest winner's cheque of just a thousand pounds, but by the end of the month the advertisements had ceased. They were never to recommence.

Ring Pools never featured as one of the members of the Football Pools Promoters Association which was set up in 1937 to ensure consistent standards and fairness. Ring Pools was even outgunned in the celebrity stakes when Ambrose, the famous bandleader whose own life story had preceded James's in the *News of the World,* was used by Littlewoods in competition with his one-time friend; and he was followed up by the Earl of Lonsdale and the Countess of Oxford and Asquith! The big battalions simply rolled over small fry; James's dreams of financial security at the stroke of a pen quickly evaporated. Ring Pools folded within a few months, leaving unpaid bills and debts. The coupons blocking James's garage were quietly burnt.

It was not the end of the world for Alex, however. He had a sports reporting job with the same *News of the World* which would keep him involved with the game, though it was hardly the sort of life he had envisaged for himself.

The following season, 1938/39, he applied to the Football Association to be allowed to enter football management. No job was specified but coaching and training positions were certainly on offer, if he were free to take them. The FA was now in a perfect position to extract vengeance. James, it was declared, had been tainted by his association with football pools; 'We are unable to accede to his request.' He was banned from football indefinitely.

His life now settled down, for a time, into a predictable routine, established in his football days. Saturday afternoon was still match day, albeit in the press box. After that, it was a drink in town, a night-club or a film. Sunday was taken up with golf, as indeed were most other days of the week. The venue was the South Herts Golf-club, not far from his home, where James was great friends with the golf professional there, Steve Thomas:

> We had a regular routine when he was playing, which continued when he retired. He would come up each afternoon to play, but on a Monday morning he would sit in the golf shop and watch me making clubs and he would read all the papers. He would also

chat to people coming in and out and relax. The club was a
home from home, really – probably spent more time there than
at home! He was a reasonable little golfer, quite useful. His
proudest day was when he won the Harry Varden trophy here
in 1938 [Varden had been the professional at the club and had
brought Thomas to South Herts from the North Middlesex
Golf-club, which had been the Arsenal golf-club for many
years.] The Varden trophy was awarded to the best scratch
golfer of the year. The winner got a little replica and I think he
thought more of that than he did the football medals – but then
he gave most of those away.

He introduced a lot of Arsenal boys to the club, especially the
younger ones. He brought the Comptons up here and I gave Denis
Compton his first golf lesson. Alex worshipped young Compton.
He would ring him up on match days to get him out of bed
because Denis was a lazy so-and-so! Absent-minded but totally
without nerves. Alex took an interest in him and coached him
from the very start. He said he was one who listened.

In fact, Peggy still put up such younger players at their home, and
it was through them that Alex James kept in touch with affairs at
Arsenal.

Arsenal had won the League in 1938, the season following
James's retirement, but with the lowest total of points since before
the First World War. However, the problem of his 'successor' had
proved an insuperable one. A succession of men had been tried
(even Cliff Bastin had been given the chance to fill his old partner's
boots) but it was not until August 1938 that Arsenal plunged into
the transfer market in a big way, spending £14,000 on Bryn Jones
– the 'new James'.

Ironically this was about the same time that James's own banishment from football was confirmed, but he must have sympathised
as he watched Jones struggle to both fit into the side and to come
to terms with the expectations a huge fee always raises. Arsenal
achieved nothing in the 1938/39 season, the first Jones played for
them, and the last before the outbreak of war. By the time it was
over, Bryn Jones's peak years had passed.

Arsenal, however, despite no longer being the supreme footballing team it once was, remained the 'glamour' club. With Allison
the arch-publicist in charge, it was always going to be in the news:

in 1938 some of the players even starred in a full-length feature film, *The Arsenal Stadium Mystery*, for which Allison received £500 while the Arsenal stars earned some £50 a week each. Indeed, so glamorous were the players thought to be that some, like Eddie Hapgood, were even considered possible film-stars. Hapgood was apparently spotted while on tour in Europe in 1938 and recommended to MGM by a Polish girl name Jacie Rotawanda who, according to Hapgood, 'always popped up from nowhere and attached herself to Arsenal when we went on tour.' Though Hapgood never actually made the break into films, this opportunity demonstrates how widespread Arsenal's reputation had become by the late 1930s. Famous across Europe, admired and emulated, they had come to epitomise English football and its strengths: strong, fast, dashing and thoroughly professional.

And it was this international reputation that was to provide Alex James with his footballing swansong. In the summer of 1939, as Arsenal set off for a summer tour of Scandinavia and James resigned himself to another summer whiling away the hours in Steve Thomas's golf shop, there came an offer of a coaching post – all the way from Poland! His daughter, Patsy, explained:

> With the ban on his being involved in any kind of football (they even stopped him from playing in a charity match at Northampton) he jumped at the chance. No question about hating travelling now . . .
>
> It was a contract to coach all the top players in Poland, although who had arranged it was a mystery. No one really knew, except that they were keen to have him and he was keen to go.

In fact, the Polish Football Association had arranged for James to give a series of training courses, three in all, each one of two weeks' duration. James was to be put up at the Academy of Physical Training in Warsaw and his schedule of lectures was to start in the second week in June, each one taking place between 4.30 and 6.30 in the evening.

In addition, he was to have a series of articles printed in *Przeglad Sportowy* – the *Sporting Press* of Poland – outlining his ideas, comments and criticisms. 'Alex James Speaks', 'Alex James: Fitness, fitness and again fitness', 'News from Alex James's Camp' – some of the headlines would have read in English. They accompanied photos of him in action, or lecturing, or with his arms over the shoulders of Poland's top players. One even showed him incongruously swinging a golf-club in rather thick grass: Poland had no golf-courses, though apparently no one had warned him. However, the whole project was a gratifying boost to his morale.

What was unusual was that he wrote home so regularly! That was rare. Mum always tells of the time she found a postcard in his jacket-pocket, an embroidered one from France – Roses of Picardy – which he had bought for her on one of his trips to Paris but had forgotten to send. He had used it as a betting marker instead. She always said that 'Roses of Picardy' was her favourite song after that!

But he seemed really buoyed up by the Polish trip. There was a suggestion that a lady journalist who was assigned to translate his articles and so on rather fell for him, but we don't know how far that went. She is supposed to have warned him about the invasion by Germany . . .

His training stint in Poland put James briefly at the heart of the rapidly expanding European game. The Poles were an extremely keen footballing nation, with in 1939 an estimated 880 clubs (and some 100,000 players) taking part in the game.

The game had really blossomed with the establishment of the Free Polish State in 1919. Prior to that, football had been a popular sport but running leagues and clubs was problematical while Russia controlled large areas of the country and frowned on any indiginous organisations. Still, certain brave Englishmen working in industry in Lodz had established a club before the First World War and, in 1911, Aberdeen had passed through on tour and had played Cracow – Polish football could thus draw upon British and neighbouring Austrian influences.

They had entered the World Cups of 1934 and 1938; in the latter they had taken Brazil into extra time 5-5, before losing by the odd goal in 11! And in 1936 they had even beaten England's amateur team at the Olympic games, 5-4 in front of some 20,000 fans in Italy.

James arrived on 6 June 1939, towards the end of the Polish football season, as it then ran from spring until the late autumn. Part of his job was to coach Polish coaches and younger players, but also to help the Poles prepare for the Olympic games planned for 1940. More immediately, there was a friendly international against the powerful Hungarians.

James worked closely with some of Poland's greatest players, in particular the Polish star Joseph Katúza who, as well as being the Polish team manager, was also a teacher of Polish in a secondary school.

James's reputation preceded him: the 'famous player of London's Arsenal' was warmly welcomed, praised in the sporting press, and everything he said listened to with great respect. Not that James was much of a theorist. He soon dispensed with the blackboard and the tactical lectures, preferring instead to get out on to the pitch and try and demonstrate what he thought was important: a sensible course of action as his Polish was non-existent and the translator (whether the smitten lady journalist or Joseph Katúza himself) found his thick Glaswegian accent a formidable barrier.

James managed to play in at least two matches. Planning to jog about and observe for 15 minutes in the first game against a Hungarian club side, Szedi, he eventually stayed on for the full 90, thoroughly enjoying himself. (Though he admitted later in an interview that, as he had not played properly for almost two years, he felt the next morning as though he had 'been run through a mangle'.)

True to form, he had little praise to offer the eager Poles, preferring instead to castigate the players for their lack of fitness, of speed and stamina and, above all, of organisation. In one match, a 4-4 draw against the same Hungarian side, he was critical of their covering in defence, especially at corners where a goal had been conceded. Moreover, he was particularly hard on those players who were reluctant to release the ball quickly enough – too much dribbling!

For their part, the players were shocked at how hard he made them work; instead of four times around the training pitch it was ten, fifteen times and, reading between the lines (for Poles are traditionally diplomatic in whatever they commit to print, even in sports papers), it would seem that as the international against the Hungarians approached, the Polish observers thought James had pushed the squad too hard. There were polite suggestions that he had tried to cram too much into too short a time. A lot of water would have to flow down the Vistula before Poland could hope to match the English at their natural game, it was suggested.

As he prepared to leave, however, the press were fulsome in their praise: they declared he would be remembered for a long time to come and that they would always be in his debt. It was even hinted that they would want him back, perhaps on a regular basis . . .

James sailed home on 11 August, after having spent almost 10 months as a top national team coach. Two weeks after he had gone, the Poles met the Hungarians and won 4-2, having fought back from 2-1 down at half-time, showing unexpected strength and stamina!

Four days after that, Germany entered Poland and, as the Polish *History of the Football Association* puts it, 'the long night of occupation began.' Patsy remembers:

Dad tried to contact some of the people he had met there after the war, including the lady journalist, but he never saw any of them again. Many of them had been officers in the Polish Army, so it was very sad. A couple of Polish airmen called by during the war who remembered him during that time, but that was about all. He brought back a box of photos and a silver cigarette box they had presented to him. And young Alec had a little Polish pennant on his bedroom wall for years afterwards.

And so the serious side of Alex James's football career ended. It was a strange twist that it should have been Poland that had asked him to help them and teach them. As a boy in Bellshill, he and Hughie had often scrapped in the playgrounds with the children of immigrants who had come looking for work in the coal-mines, mimicking their accents and their Catholic affiliations – immigrants all the way from Lithuania and Poland.

19

Finale

One of my first decisions on my appointment as Secretary-manager of Arsenal in 1947 was to bring Alec James back to Highbury in a staff capacity . . . and he took an intense delight in trying to coach some of our younger players. George Allison, *Allison Calling*

WITH THE WAR over, the Football Association lifted the ban on James's involvement in football and he returned, inevitably, to Arsenal.

Tom Whittaker, for long the Arsenal trainer, took control of the team in 1947. After the Arsenal of Chapman and Allison would now come the Arsenal of Whittaker, and it was fitting that the man who Chapman had said would be the greatest trainer in the world should now become the leader to take Arsenal into the modern era. For if Chapman had been the brain and Allison the voice of Arsenal, then Tom Whittaker was surely its heart and soul.

His record in the seven seasons between 1947 and 1953 would equal Allison's and Chapman's: Champions in 1948 and 1953, Cup-winners in 1950 and Finalists in 1952 – and not once during this period out of the top six in the First Division.

Whittaker, like his predecessors, was a man of many parts. During the war he started off like so many footballers as an RAF PT instructor, but his special engineering skills soon led him into crucial repair work on crashed aircraft; he became a squadron leader and for his secret work prior to the D-Day landings he received, in 1945, the MBE.

The contrast with Alec James's war record could not have been starker. In 1939, having managed to scramble out of Poland, he was an occasional journalist; he was in his late thirties and apparently in no danger of being called up. He was, in any case, a reluctant participant in the war. Patsy, who was still at home, recalls:

When the war started everybody in the street had to take a turn at fire-watching; we were all very keen at that stage. You had a dustbin lid and a hammer to bang it with! But when it came to Dad's turn, he was nowhere to be found. Up the golf-course, naturally!

So when he got called up in 1942 it came as something of a shock. We could see the joke but he certainly didn't. He did his basic training in Congleton, under canvas and hated every minute of it. He was put in the Royal Artillery and was in an emergency ack-ack unit at first, racing into areas that had been bombed – a sort of morale-booster.

James eventually left Congleton and tried to 'work his passage' at the Kempston rehabilitation centre. Allan Bartlett, who was there at the same time, recalled:

It was full of people from all sorts of regiments, a clearing-house where people were sent for assessment. You were examined regularly, given physiotherapy if you had been injured, etc. There was a lot of shamming, people limping up to the main gates on their way out on leave, then sprinting for the bus!

James, I seem to remember, enjoyed a totally undisciplined sort of existence: he really was the scruffiest of soldiers, seldom seemed to have shaved, except once a week when he went up to London to appear on the Tommy Trinder show at the Palladium. But he seemed to get away with anything because people worshipped him. He was Alex James.

Patsy recalled he had even acquired his own batman:

We got a telegram that he was passing through King's Cross Station and we went to meet him, hurried down there, and it was absolute chaos with soldiers and sailors everywhere and, all of a sudden, we saw a little troop marching along and there was Daddy, with a little chap struggling along behind him carrying two kitbags, one in his right hand and one in his left! Daddy was just strolling! The little man was a Mancunian Italian who was even smaller than Daddy. He put the kitbags down and said, 'Cup of tea, Alex?' There were all these poor blokes queueing for tea but not Alex James. That little man idolised him.

James had failed to find a way out of the Army and was now Gunner James No. 11428681 Royal Artillery Maritime Division, stationed at Shoeburyness. Alec Junior remembers:

He'd heard it was easier than the normal Royal Artillery and had managed to get himself transferred there, somehow. Merchant ships were armed with ack-ack guns and when they put a Bofors gun on board they would man them with Army crews from the Royal Artillery. But Dad never went to sea. He was too old, in his forties. Instead, he got himself permanently assigned to cleaning duties, stores, that sort of thing, but he took it all as a gag. He hated uniforms of any kind, likewise authority. And he was able, for most of the time, to get away with things. There were pictures of him posing in uniform with a latrine brush instead of a rifle. Not that he cleaned the toilets – he paid someone else for that.

He would get weekend passes whenever he wanted and travel up to London to report matches for the *News of the World*. I can remember seeing him at a wartime international in full gunner's uniform but wearing 10-guinea Saxone shoes because he was excused boots. He was excused just about everything. He had bumps on his forehead and so he was excused wearing a beret. He had tender feet, hence the boots. He was even excused the NAAFI food because it upset his stomach. There was a whelk stall at Southend that used to save him things specially and someone went to fetch them for him. He had a chitty for everything and he was the only man I knew who had a plastic cap badge so he wouldn't have to clean it!

There were times when things grew difficult, however, but James had the wherewithal and the luck to wriggle out of trouble. His friend, Steve Thomas, has stories from that time:

A new officer arrived who thought he was getting too much time off, and who stopped the weekend passes. Then it was discovered that the base had no bicycle pumps for the bicycles. Alex knew a cycle manufacturer from the golf-club – Scott someone. He got on the phone: 'Scotty! We need some pumps here!' And a few days later, two dozen pumps. And his weekend passes began again.

James settled down at Shoeburyness for the duration. As men came and went, he remained, an oddball fixture, someone to be glimpsed as he played the occasional game of football on the recreation ground. According to Patsy, he was usually up to rather more resourceful games, however:

> He got in with a local farmer and somehow got an old car. Where he got the petrol from during wartime no one asked, but he turned up in Barnet with the car stacked with vegetables: turnips, cauliflowers, half the farm! You can imagine what the neighbours thought. Even without the car his kitbag would be stuffed with food. He was always into some fiddle or other . . .

At home in Barnet, there had been changes. In 1939 his wife Peggy had given birth to a second son, Andrew, while their first son, Alec, had suddenly taken himself off to join the merchant navy. Patsy described it:

> One minute he was at home at school, the next he was joining up. He went to Liverpool and we didn't hear from him for some time. And then suddenly he turned up, smoking, with a bit of a beard. With the war having started he didn't want to go in as a cadet as he could have done; instead, he went in as an able seaman, roughing it. Our hero!
>
> He was probably reacting against the private school business and the sort of life he had led. He wanted to go and prove himself, not always be in Dad's shadow – and he certainly proved something.

Alec explained:

> I think Dad was a little jealous. He always found it hard to let the barriers down between us, and now I had done what he had always wanted to do. I had been to America, the land of Jimmy Cagney and George Raft. I had American clothes and I'd brought silk stockings for Mother and I was only 15. I'd beaten him to it!
>
> During the War Tommy Trinder had a programme on the radio broadcasting to the Forces and Dad had come on and sent me a message: 'Haven't heard from you for a while; hope you're all

right, you big stiff.' You see, still having a go, because I was taller and bigger – a big stiff!

But all the time I was in the merchant marine, especially when we had Scottish crews, there would be people who would come up to me and say: 'You're wee Alec's son!' and they would look at me as if I was God. Second-hand hero-worship!

At the end of the war when Alec Junior decided to join the police force, the gulf between father and son appeared as unbridgeable as ever.

Because in his book, you never joined up voluntarily! You were mad if you did that. And the police of all things! I had only been in a few months and he asked me why I hadn't got my gold watch yet. Because when he had been a boy, back before the First War, the police in Glasgow had been in cahoots with the bookies. They were as bad as the criminals. You could say he had a biased opinion of the police!

James's war experiences were in complete contrast to those of his ex-playing colleagues. Like Whittaker, most had joined the RAF as PT instructors. They were still the 'glamour boys', and many of them were able to take part in the extensive wartime football activities, involving internationals and League competitions. There were so many Arsenal men in the RAF that they could, and often did, form their own eleven. James, being too old, missed out on the fun but, with the war over, he rejoined men like George Male, Jack Crayston and the two Compton brothers, Leslie and Denis, as Whittaker set about rebuilding the Arsenal 'family'.

Whittaker was James's closest friend at Highbury and it was for him that James reserved his highest praise:

'He was more than just a trainer. The manager of a club has nothing like the intimate contact with the players that the trainer has. That is where Tom stands out,' James wrote in 1937. 'Tom has been worth more to Arsenal than any other player . . .'

Whittaker's years in charge were years of battling against and triumphing over the odds. He bought Joe Mercer in 1947, luring him back from the brink of retirement and making him captain – a key appointment:

'Only one man – Alex James – has contributed more than Joe Mercer,' wrote Bernard Joy in *Forward Arsenal*, 'to Arsenal's greatness.' And from 1947 until he broke his leg in 1954 and was finally forced into retirement, Mercer led Arsenal by example, courage and skill, truly the inspiration of the side just as James had been before the War.

Fortunately, James was able to play his part during those exciting years. When not working with George Male at Hendon with the Juniors and the Third Team, he was lending his expert advice and assistance to men like Jimmy Logie, upon whom the 'James' mantle had fallen, Alex Forbes (who even wore James's boots for luck during the 1950 Cup run) and Arthur Milton – and many more. James was still not an orthodox coach: 'His method was probably not according to the book because he was impatient if the youngsters made mistakes. But they thought much of him.'

He even managed to turn out for representative Arsenal sides in testimonials. In 1949 he played at Crystal Palace for Ronnie Rooke's Eleven versus Tommy Lawton's Eleven, and in 1950 for a team known as 'Ancient Lights' which included old friends like Wilf Copping, Joe Hulme, Eddie Hapgood and Bernard Joy.

His last match, in 1951, was an impromptu appearance for Arsenal in a benefit match for George Cox against Horsham. Bob Wall recalls:

On the journey to Horsham where the match was to be played Alex asked, 'Can I turn out for a little while as it's for George's benefit fund?'

You could sense the crowd's pleasure at the news of Alex's appearance. He played the first half and, when he came in at the interval, he murmured to me, 'Well, Bob, if that's modern football I've had it. I know nothing about the game whatever. I couldn't live in that speed for five minutes.'

In fact, Alex was brilliant. His wing partner Don Bennett, who also played cricket for Middlesex, confessed to me afterwards 'Bob, it was uncanny the way Alex kept finding me. If he can play like that now he must have been fantastic in his prime.'

Sadly, by 1951, Alex James was already a sick man.

A year later he entered the Brompton Hospital where cancer was diagnosed, though neither he nor his children were told. They thought it was tuberculosis. The surgeon, Sir Bryce Thomas, removed a lung and James made a partial recovery but, as Tom Whittaker observed, he refused to take things easy:

> I remember the day he came to me not many weeks before he went into hospital for the last time, complaining of pain and it seemed like old times in that whenever Alec had anything the matter with him he would immediately come to us.

James was finally taken seriously ill at home and was rushed into a local hospital:

> He'd never been in a general ward before: a big ward with 30, 40 men all together. When we went to see him he had a look on his face, like, what have you done to me! Good God, get me out of here! Mum got on to the Arsenal and the next thing he was in the Royal Northern Hospital in a private room, a TV – all he wanted. Unfortunately, a male nurse at the general hospital had told us – luckily, not Dad – that there was no hope.

Whittaker was a constant visitor during the last weeks, even though Arsenal were heading for the championship and things were hectic at Highbury. Indeed, James's room had a constant stream of visitors passing through it: footballers, boxers, sportsmen of all kinds, and many friends. James held court, bantered, even hustled for Cup Final tickets. His old friend Steve Thomas remembered:

> I'd already got tickets for the game, but Alex insisted he could get better ones so he got on the phone to people – David Jack up in Middlesbrough I remember – 'Hey, Davie! I need some tickets!' And on Cup Final morning I got a phone call from him; he'd got me better tickets. I went down there a week later to say thanks, and I left money in his suit in the wardrobe and I said cheerio! It was the last time I saw him.

Tom Whittaker was almost the last person to speak to him before he died.

> Everybody played ball and kept the secret from Alec and he never knew until almost the day he died. I was with him one afternoon

when the wee man said, through the dope they were giving him
to ease the pain, 'Tom, I'm dying . . . and I'm afraid.' I consoled
him and he calmed. With a smile he said, 'It's been a fine life,
Tom. I've loved every minute of it.'

I was with him, together with Billy Milne, until a few minutes
before he died and nobody will know just what the death of the
gallant little man with the big heart meant to me.

Alec James died on 1 June 1953, the day before the Coronation of
Elizabeth II.

Almost exactly four years later, in June 1957, Hughie Gallacher,
burdened with personal problems, walked in front of a train as it
thundered over a crossing near Gateshead. As John Rafferty put it:
'Life had only been tolerable when he was playing football.'

James, by contrast, had always found life both on and off the field
a great deal of fun. Unlike that other great Scots footballer, Bill
Shankly, James did not consider football 'more important than life
and death'. It had always been very much a means to an end – a
way of earning sufficient money to lead a comfortable life. That he
failed ultimately to set himself up successfully once his playing
days were over proved irrelevant: he died in middle age before the
harsh reality of his parlous financial state became too difficult to
cope with.

If James had been playing now he could, of course, have lived a
comfortable life in retirement – with his ready wit and his instant
recognisability he would have been the perfect football 'celebrity'
television pundit, sponsored for life by companies anxious to pour
advertising revenue into the game.

Such commercial opportunities were not open to him, nor to any
footballer in the 1940s and 1950s. The view that he was well paid
enough over the course of his career and that society owed him nothing more is, perhaps, a valid one. But it cannot be denied that
James's personality and presence had been a source of amusement,
fascination and joy for millions who thronged through the turnstiles
to see him play during Arsenal's golden period. Few other great
players were so much larger than life as James, and football as a
commercial entertainment thrives on such unique characters –
indeed they are more significant as milestones in football's history
than Cup Finals or internationals.

James certainly deserved far more by way of financial security than he ultimately managed. For there can be no doubting the extent to which he was genuinely loved by all who came in contact with him, not least by those among the Highbury crowds who came to know him simply as 'Alex' or 'wee Alec'. As the Scots writer put it after the 1928 England-Scotland international: 'It was easy to be pleasant when life, as represented by a wonderful game, went by like a song.'

James, despite his 'commercial' image, was a genius who expressed himself through a wonderful game. In doing so he made those present on the terraces feel good to be alive. Their undying affection for 'wee Alex' was the result of a deep and lasting gratitude.

Bibliography

Allison Calling   George Allison
Arsenal From the Heart   Bob Wall
Arsenal 1886/1986   Soar and Tyler
Association Football: 4 Vols Ed. Fabian and Green
Cliff Bastin Remembers   Cliff Bastin
Football Ambassador   Eddie Hapgood
Football Grounds of England and Wales   Simon Inglis
Football Who's Who   Ed. Frank Johnson
Football Encyclopedia   Ed. Frank Johnson
Football Fireside Book   Ed. Terence Delaney
Forward Arsenal   Bernard Joy
Footballer's Companion   Ed. Brian Glanville
Great Britain Between The Wars   C. L. Mowat
Great Masters of Scottish Football   Hugh Taylor
Herbert Chapman on Football   Herbert Chapman
Herbert Chapman   Stephen Studd
Kirkcaldy Walkabouts   Kirkcaldy Civic Society
My Story   Matt Busby
My Preston Yesterdays   Kathlyn Davenport
One Hundred Years at Deepdale   Harry Berry & Geoff Allman
One Hundred Years of Scottish Football   John Rafferty
Raith Rovers – a History   John Litster
Shankly   Bill Shankly
Soccer   David Jack
Soccer Tactics   Bernard Joy
Soccer from the Inside   Jimmy Seed
Soccer Nemesis   Brian Glanville
Soccer Revolution   Willie Meisl
The Scottish Footballer   Bob Crampsey
The Scots   Moray McLaren

Selfridges Gordon Honeycombe
Whittaker's Arsenal Story Tom Whittaker

Newspaper files consulted include those of the: Kirkcaldy Times; Lancashire Daily Post; Glasgow Evening Times; Bellshill Observer; Daily Mail; News of the World; Topical Times; Thomson's Weekly News.

Index